Pitch Craft

Pitch Craft

The Writer's Guide to Getting Agented, Published, and Paid

LAURA GOODE

TEN SPEED PRESS
California | New York

For all those who have no choice but to write

CONTENTS

Why does the talented student of writing stop? It is usually the imagination, turned to creating a story in which you are a failure, and all you have done has failed, and you are made out to be the fraud you've feared you are. You can imagine the story you might tell, or you can imagine this other story—both will be extraordinarily detailed, but only one will be something you can publish. The other will freeze you in place, in a private theater of pain that seats one. These writers were—are, in many cases—people who know how to write. What they don't know is how to become unstuck. How to leave that theater they made for themselves, how to stop telling themselves the story that freezes them. I discovered I needed to teach not just how to write, but how to keep writing. How to face up to who you think is listening. Is the person listening more important than you? Or is the story you would tell more important than you? I was teaching how to stand up and leave that room in your mind so you can go and write—and live.

—Alexander Chee
How to Write an Autobiographical Novel

The Art of Losing
Is Hard as Fuck to Master

The story of this book must begin with my most devastating professional failure.

My life as a writer has gone like this. First, like almost anyone who would ever purchase this book, I was a bookish kid. Then I studied English and creative writing in college and earned a master of fine arts (MFA) degree in writing in 2008. (We will *very* much return to the subject of my MFA program later.) I published a young adult novel in 2011. I released a feature film in 2013. I birthed a human baby in 2014. I published a collection of poetry in 2016. And I birthed another human baby in 2018.

Between 2010 and 2018, I wrote a novel and an essay collection, and worked with two different literary agents to sell them. The novel went out on about five submission rounds; the essay collection went out on about three or four. Every round ratcheted up my hopes. In 2016 we almost sold the essay collection, but the editor who'd expressed such fervent interest ghosted us. In 2017 we almost sold the novel, but the editor who'd expressed such fervent interest turned out to be too junior to convince her bosses to fund the acquisition.

The waiting, the hoping, the lack of control, and the ceaseless rejections were excruciating. And they continued for *years.*

Between age three, when I started stapling construction paper to printer paper and writing books, and my early thirties, the prospect of giving up on my dream never really crossed my mind. My writing career taught me how to steel myself against rejection (another topic we'll revisit), and I have a certain measure of natural hubris.

Somewhere around the fiftieth rejection of the novel, though, my confidence wavered. What if the book never sold? What if I never sold another book at all? Absent the delusional confidence of my twenties, when talent was still all potential and a life was still more future than past, I got even better acquainted with hard truths inherent to the writing life: Plenty of people give it their all and never get a lucky break. Talent and hard work aren't always enough.

Amid those rejections, failure haunted me. It woke and tossed me at three in the morning. It distracted me when I tried to work. Why wouldn't either of my books, the books I'd written and revised and sent out over and over again, the books that were now on their second agent, the books I'd humbled myself before, the books I'd plunged into the depths of myself for—why wouldn't they sell? Those books were my heart. They brought me to and over the brink of tears every time I thought about them. What the fuck did I have to do to make them *enough*?

There was no answer to be found. Every time I circled around these questions, I found myself in a new grip of torture, goose-stepping to the sickening drumbeat of *I want, I want, I want.* I was future-tripping. I was placing all of my happiness, my self-worth, my fulfillment, my entire purpose as a writer—something I'd declared myself to be as early as age five—around the corner of my next achievement: a place so lonely and ambitious I could never get there.

I was as professionally miserable as I'd ever been, and there was greater suffering to come.

Eventually, the novel had been rejected by maybe 100 or 150 editors, and the essay collection by 80 or 100. The message was clear: The entire industry was seizing its don't-miss opportunity to pass on these books.

After we'd withdrawn the novel, I got a wincing, tenderly worded email from my second, now former agent saying, hey, I don't really want to represent nonfiction anymore, and I think it's time to take the essay collection off the market too.

What this meant was, two weeks before my thirty-fifth birthday, as I sat in my house with two children under five who seemed to expect me to feed them multiple times a day, I was confronting the cold fact that the work I'd spent the previous eight years pouring my entire heart into . . . was done. These two books were dead. They wouldn't be published. They would not deliver a financial return on the investment of my time and skill. I would never tweet a victorious screenshot of their deal announcement. I would never discuss these books' allusions and influences with audiences of readers. I would never open their quarterly earnings reports.

My brain, medic to my ego, tried to bandage the wound with humor: I imagined what I could ever tweet about this major turning point in my career.

Some personal news! I'm cutting my losses, going back to square one, shitting my pants, and crying on a beach. My baby won't sleep *and I've just dumped eight years of my professional life down the drain! *squee**

Is this thing on??? I've made a life-changing discovery: This might just be the kind of bitterness that makes people mean to their children! Anybody looking for a poet/producer?

I've been sitting on my hands until I could make this public, but: I have failed! spectacularly! in! multiple! genres!

The truth I was struggling to accept—raw, painful, unfunny—was: Many, many lovingly, skillfully crafted, fervently hoped-for books are never, ever published. And my two would be among these permanent casualties.

(You're like: Soooo I bought this book to figure out how to publish, and now you're regaling me with your greatest publishing *failures?*

I know. I know. Read on.)

• • • • •

When I tell you I was devastated? I was on the floor. I was panicking about the story I was already telling myself about this event: In this story, I had failed at my most closely held dream, my aspirations were dust, and hope and faith themselves were mirages. I wavered in and out of depression.

I was grieving, and the best thing I did for myself in that process was to recognize that I was grieving. I gave myself permission to grieve.

The primary way I grieved was to go walking in the woods near my house, on the same three-mile loop, four or five times a week. I gave myself permission to listen only to *The West Wing Weekly* podcast until I felt better, because I have viewed *The West Wing* upward of one hundred times, my elder son is named after its fictional president, and I'm a freak like that. This podcast was the safest space I could imagine, where I knew what was coming, and I knew it would be pleasurable to me.

The other way I grieved was through writing stories, the same way I process everything. In my churning frustration throughout the eight years of not selling these books, I poured furious effort into my pitching practice. Charged with supporting children, with no book advance in the bank, I took the gloves off this practice: I literally could not afford to write for compliments or retweets, and the assertiveness and frequency of my pitches reflected this. My minutes were measured in childcare dollars, and they *had* to make a return. So, during this era, when both my children and I were young and hungry, I pitched and published a lot of essays—in *ELLE, Catapult, New Republic, Glamour, Refinery29,* and anywhere else that paid. The endorphin hits of these bylines gave me the encouragement to continue writing amid the crushing defeat of my books.

As I pitched, I gradually developed a pitching procedure for myself. I scoured X/Twitter for pitch calls and personal connections, and the structure of my emails to editors gained a kind of familiarity. It dawned on me that—even though I was, in my own current estimation, a no-talent garbage fire destined for a life of broke, bitter obscurity—I had published two books; held full-time reporting jobs; written, produced, funded, and distributed an independent film; worked with two literary agents and a film distribution agent; written for a vibrant bouquet of magazines; and taught the craft of writing everywhere from maximum-security prisons to elementary school classrooms. For better or worse, I had amassed journeywoman experience as a writer.

I was certain that there were more qualified pitching experts for writers out there, but I just couldn't seem to find them. Then I wondered why, in the two years I had spent in a top MFA program with a nearly six-figure price tag, no one had breathed a word about how to pitch a story in a manner that might compel another literary professional to pay me for that skilled labor. In almost every vocation, the tuition of a graduate degree is offset by future earnings. One invests in graduate school with the expectation that it will increase one's future earning potential in the field. If a graduate student pays in tuition for a writing program more than many Americans earn in a year, it seems reasonable to expect, if retrospectively, that this program might have devoted even 5 percent of its curriculum to the question of making a living as a writer. My MFA curriculum made no such pretense, let alone promise. I know this because no one offered me a class on how to build an effective author website and online presence, query an agent, cold-pitch an editor, negotiate rates, read a contract, or manage any of writing's other business concerns. Yet these mechanisms are also how books are born.

Looking back, I see this absence as criminal, a hose job of epic proportions. I was taught to scan, to critique, to revise, to review—why was I not taught to *pitch*? It felt so procedural: I had this nagging feeling that, after making the rounds of multiple genres, I could come up with a template for pitching . . . well, just about anything.

In late 2016, I interviewed the essayist Chloe Caldwell at Green Apple Books in San Francisco, and she stayed the weekend at my house. Chloe is breezy, brilliant, a dead ringer for a young Stevie Nicks, and a stone-cold hustler who's published five spellbinding books without a college degree. I'd always admired her gumption, her focus, and her disdain for the charted path; where so many of my MFA friends were adjunct teaching for pennies, for years I'd watched Chloe teach online writing classes, from desirable locations, that seemed to sell out in a blink.

> "Chloe," I said. "Who do you know who teaches pitching?"
>
> "What do you mean?" she asked.
>
> "You know, the email you send to the editor saying *I want to write this story, here's why and how*," I said. "Who teaches that?"
>
> "I have no idea," Chloe said. "I just taught myself."
>
> "But don't you think that would be pretty straightforward to structure into, like, a six-week class?" I asked. "Like, Week 1: author website and bio. Week 2: how to pitch a short-form essay to an editor. Week 3: querying literary agents. You know?"
>
> "*You* should teach that," Chloe said. "I'm gonna give you an email address."

The email address directed me to the digital magazine *Catapult*. I spent about a month banging everything I knew about the literary industry into a seventy-page document. About a month after that, I started teaching "How to Pitch Anything" as one of the writing classes offered by the Catapult publishing company.

.   .   .   .

I went into the first class the way I go everywhere: overprepared out of fear of being underprepared. I was ready to offer tips. I was ready to serve up tricks. I was ready to make *action plans*.

It took me about thirty minutes of witnessing the sheer

vulnerability and terror of the students before me to realize that the tips, tricks, and action plans were necessary, but so was a deep engagement with the psychology of rejection, perfectionism, and fear of failure—all feelings I was intimately familiar with at that particular moment. And in this way, I realized "how to survive rejection" *had* to be a part of any pitching practice. Rejection had, after all, almost killed me. This clarity lingered with me: On the subject of surviving rejection, if on nothing else, I was utterly confident about my qualifications. *That* was something I could teach.

It became clearer with every class meeting that teaching pitching was synonymous with teaching how to *perform confidence*. My task was to teach my students how to walk into a room, literal or digital, and convince a stranger that they had an original, actionable idea. I taught them that if they could hatch that idea, make an argument for it, and thoughtfully select a target for that idea's argument, they deserved to be paid for that labor. I taught them that to be treated like a professional—acknowledged, taken seriously, paid—they first needed to regard themselves that way. It was striking, though not at all surprising, to witness how skeptical the marginalized—queer, trans, and nonbinary people; differently abled people; people of color; people born outside the United States; white women—were that anyone might treat them like professionals. Confidence became the linchpin of my pitching pedagogy: Shoot your shot, and let your curiosity and ambition speak louder than your fear. My theory about confidence, which I tell students again and again, is that you don't actually have to feel it. All you have to do is project it.

What I have internalized for myself through teaching others is the difference between a submission and a pitch. You can see it in the gesticulations of the words themselves: A submission lies prone, while a pitch acts kinetic. A submission says, *Please pick me, I'll be waiting.* A pitch says, *Catch me or you'll miss the ball.* A submission is passive; a pitch, active. I am so tired of the artistic narrative of a pretty girl being discovered in a soda shop. A *professional* is not discovered; she refuses to be ignored, to go unheard. If you cannot have an idea and summarize it effectively to a stranger, if you cannot argue for your own argument, if you cannot locate a story in your own tangled knot of pretty words, if you cannot identify an opportunity and shoot your well-aimed shot at it, then you have no business calling yourself any kind of professional writer. A career doesn't just sit there like a gift to be unwrapped. You have to wind up and throw. Drop the ball. Pick it up. Throw again.

Even as my impostor syndrome conspired with my nineties gifted-child syndrome to make me feel like both a fraud and a failure as an author, as a teacher, I watched my students take my pitching principles out into the world and find bylines, book deals, and, best of all, belief in themselves. My battered ego, as it turns out, was paying dividends in my ability to offer empathetic and informed stories from the trenches.

I rooted for my students and came to love them as I ranted to them that a career in the arts or humanities is a war of attrition and that their job was to figure out a way not to give up, for longer than they thought they could stand it. I tried to convince them— paradoxically, while also teaching them how to sell their work— that love of recognition cannot motivate you more than love of the daily practice of commanding language, because nothing and especially not external recognition will ever sustain you more than love of the craft will.

When I said this often enough to be forced to listen to myself, it got a little easier to believe it. To keep showing up for my own practice. To find more daily experiences of joy within it. This—walking in the woods, giving myself permission to grieve, teaching and practicing, showing up and feeling an increasing sense of responsibility to model how to keep showing up—brought me back to life. I started writing a new book and guarded its process fiercely.

I taught seven online rounds of the class with Catapult and two with the Minneapolis-based literary center The Loft, and meanwhile, one of my Catapult students—I can still only really tell this story with an incredulous vocal fry—told me that he was a program head at Stanford and that he wanted me to teach a version of my pitching class there?! To be honest, when this student told me he was the director of the Program in Feminist, Gender, and Sexuality Studies at Stanford, it's possible that I didn't entirely believe him. Part of me was like, you mean, Stanford . . . University? In Palo Alto? California? Part of me was like, okay, buddy, sure you are. In all honesty, I half-suspected he was generously wording his title with the intention of making a pass at me.

Maybe his job sounded like the kind of job that exists only in heaven; maybe I didn't quite trust that I'd heard him right; or maybe, obviously, what he was proposing sounded so wildly appealing that it became terrifying, so fresh on the heels of lacerating, faith-shaking disappointment. How could I find time to teach at Stanford when I was extremely busy failing at everything?

The student kept following up. His name is Adrian, and he is witty, brilliant, and kind. My arrogant disbelief that there existed a professional feminist in the San Francisco Bay Area whom I didn't know already was dispelled when I ran into him at a mutual friend's party about two weeks later. There I confirmed not only that Professor Adrian Daub was telling the unvarnished truth about his position, but also that he was married and gay.

So I, uh. I found the time.

In fall 2017, basically as a guest speaker, I taught a pilot version of the pitching class for humanities PhD candidates and postdoctoral fellows. It went well, and I was hired to teach a full credited quarter of the pitching class in winter 2019. I got all fired up about a related class on the evolution of the feminist first-person essay on the internet, I proposed it to Adrian, and his program agreed to sponsor it in fall 2019.

Then—and this is where my vocal fry gets even more incredulous—at the end of May 2019, I got a call from one of Stanford's deans of the humanities? Asking me if I wanted to accept a full-year, part-time lecturer/administrator position to teach my two classes and—what the *fuck*—serve as the first director of their new Humanities Public Writing Project? In which my mandates would be to teach the craft of pitching, to facilitate mentorship and paid writing opportunities for students, and to coordinate an ongoing speaker series of visiting authors. At Stanford. University. It's actually in Stanford, California.

If I'm honest, I still have some trouble telling this part of the story; the failure is still easier to recount, perversely, than the success. Nonetheless, it happened: I got a job at this extremely famous university without ever applying. From my own lived experience, I identified a gap in graduate arts and humanities pedagogy, and Stanford thought that gap was significant enough to create a job for me to fill it.

My survivor's guilt has been loud in this job: Why should *I* get this plum position, when the line of qualified applicants is thousands deep? My lack of a PhD is conspicuous in such an august corner of the academy, and its effect double-edged: Where it probably diminishes me in the eyes of certain of my colleagues, I was also never subject to its training in deference to them. I am not particularly attached to the way things have always been done in academia. I have no allegiance whatsoever to the unpaid, cloistered, byzantine world of academic publishing. I staunchly reject elite-academic precepts of overworking to the point of self-harm, prioritizing individual achievement over community bargaining power, and muzzling one's politics until after the tenure review. I arrived at the academy as a practitioner, not a scholar, and I remain obstinately so.

It's knotty to articulate how walking away from my two dead books enabled me to teach how to write living ones. But I know this: As I grieved the loss of those books, I had to ask myself if I would keep writing even if I never published a single thing ever again. Some people might be done with writing after two books died, and I wouldn't cast any aspersions on that decision. But when I struck my inner tuning fork and asked it this about myself—would I keep writing if I never published again—the Laura inside Laura rang back and said: *Fool, of course you would. Why are you torturing yourself like this? Yes! Writing is not about capitalism for you, Laura. Writing is your spiritual mandate.*

And I know this for sure: That hard-earned note of self-knowledge has enabled in me the most serene, enveloping confidence I've ever felt. In this knowledge, I have no fear of rejection. When the only measured success is showing up to my own writing practice in earnestness, wholeheartedness, and joy, I have no reason to fear failure.

Of course, this confidence has been engendered, in part, by my teaching job relieving financial pressure on my writing job. But it also sprang forth from a deep, dark reckoning in the woods, in which I came face-to-face with the ugliest dimensions of my own narcissistic self-loathing, in which I faced the failure I feared most, and in which I not only grieved the death of my books, but ultimately also released my wrongheaded conviction that I had to *earn* worthiness and belonging through external achievement. It was in those woods that I relocated Rilke's "Must I write? I must." And I rededicated myself to the practice of building my life in accordance with that knowledge.

What I wish to convey, however improbable, is this: The story of my greatest professional failure led directly to one of my most transformative professional successes. Many of my life's most abiding and transformative truths have arrived through paradox, and paradoxically, it was only once I had located the inner resource to grieve that publishing failure that I was able to succeed in pitching and publishing new writing, and to build the external resources to teach a practice of pitching and publishing.

.   •   .   •   .

I offer you this long, strange story to demonstrate that I'm not full of shit when I say that I really do understand how hard rejection, perseverance, and literary ambition can be. I have lived through rejection. I have lived through *hundreds* of rejections. And I survived. It's possible to survive. I know how it feels to have your worst professional fear realized and still call yourself a writer after that, in good faith, with total earnestness, and with greater confidence than before. This is how I know that the name of the game here is self-sustenance and not achievement. Because, at least for the luckiest among us, being a writer is a long game.

I know, if you're reading this, that you're a writer too. Maybe you have an MFA, maybe you don't. Maybe you've never told a soul about the poems you write on your lunch break. Maybe you have a PhD, an ABD, a BA in a subject you'll never touch again, a trade certificate, or a few semesters of nontransferable credits. Maybe you got an MD because your parents wanted you to, but you've never truly given up on the screenplay in your drawer. Maybe, like a striking proportion of the students I used to teach online, you used your English major as a bridge to a JD, then spent your billable hours still dreaming of your Great American Novel. Maybe, like me, you skipped so much class in high school that it's a wonder you ever graduated. Maybe, like some of the students I used to teach in a maximum-security juvenile facility, you're working on your GED and a memoir in prison.

The point is that you're a writer, and all writers are welcome here. The point is that you're a writer, and no degree, experience, or interlocutor can apply that title to your professional identity except your own sheer nerve. A writer is a person who writes. You don't need to write every day to call yourself a writer. (Does anybody ever ask doctors if they practice medicine every day? Are plumbers required to snake pipes every goddamn day?) You don't need to earn your entire living from writing to call yourself a writer. You don't need to hold an MFA to call yourself a writer. You don't need to be published, ever, to call yourself a writer.

Know this: If you call yourself a writer, I believe you. And I hope this book can help you along the path of believing, and believing in, yourself.

Here's the really good news: You're about to get more actionable information on building a career as a writer from this book than I ever got in six years of instruction, BA to MFA, from one of the most "prestigious" writing programs in the country. I still feel pretty salty that over the course of my writing education I learned volumes about the craft of writing and nothing about the business of making a living as a writer. None of my professors, brilliant, generous, and accomplished as they were, ever taught me anything specific or actionable about how to pitch an editor, query an agent, network effectively, or generally behave like a professional in a manner that might eventually compel others to compensate me for my work.

If you write only for yourself and have no desire for audience or compensation, I salute you; hobbies are good for the health. But I want to be paid for my labor, so I had to learn how to sell it. I have found that there is a unique satisfaction, so great an aid to writing that it *is* writing, in forcing myself to compose two artful sentences that encapsulate the idea that won't leave me alone. Pitching is its own subgenre of nonfiction, applicable—essential, I argue—to an artist's work in any genre. If I can articulate what I am writing about and why, I invariably write it better.

The process of teaching myself to pitch, and its continuation into the process of teaching other writers to pitch, have reinforced to me how fiercely gatekept the literary community remains. It's revealed to me how high the walls around publishing and media can appear when you live in Tulsa, Corpus Christi, or East Palo Alto, and how indecipherable their unwritten rules can read when you don't have the privilege of a seasoned, published mentor. It's revealed to me the dire need for collective bargaining power among writers, which can coalesce only from the free and promiscuous sharing of information.

(Let me mention here where I have found seasoned, published mentors: in my formal degree programs, yes, but also in conferences I received scholarships to attend, inexpensive online classes, and, most especially, dive bars. In my experience, the constituents of America's service industry are at least as well read as those of its ivory towers.)

I contend that the best way you can spend your journey

through this book is by setting, and incrementally achieving, one actionable, manageable goal with regard to your practice of pitching and publishing. I encourage you to make this goal both specific and ambitious. A zoomed-in goal like "I'd like to pitch *Slate* a researched first-person essay on how my four-year-old son won't stop talking to Alexa" is something this material can help you build. A vague, vast goal like "I'd like to write more poetry" or "I'd like to finish the second draft of my novel," worthwhile as it is, is less actionable within the scope of these offerings.

Because I'm of the opinion that learning happens best when general, conceptual suggestions are combined with specific, experiential examples, this craft book offers tips, tricks, frequently asked questions, and templates, along with some longer meditations on how these principles have influenced my writing career. The questions my students ask most frequently guide the content of these chapters, and each chapter concludes with a relatively brief writing assignment. (Beware buying books by professors: I am brazen enough to give you homework.) These chapters and their attendant assignments cover, successively, what I've identified as the steps of building a pitch, and they're designed cumulatively to enable you to leave this reading experience with a finished pitch in hand.

I fear, as I collect these thoughts, that you might perceive me to be in cahoots with capitalism or advocating for its moral virtue—to be clear, I am not. I am simply a literary professional who classifies writing as a labor of value and who contends that if we are all forced to survive under the crushing and multiply oppressive yoke of capitalism, then those of us who devote our labor to scholarship, story, argument, and thought—particularly those of us who have historically been excluded from such vocations—

are also entitled to a living. Collectively we bargain, and together we rise.

My wish for you, dear reader, as you delve into the process of putting your work out into the world, is that you may also ask yourself these questions, and listen sincerely to your own answers:

- Would I write if I were never published at all, or ever again?
- Which rejections have protected me from what was not meant for me or prepared me for what *was* meant for me?
- Whom do I write for? Who is the audience dearest and most personal to me?
- Would the five-year-old version of me be proud of the action the adult me has taken toward my most closely held dreams? Would the eighty-five-year-old version of me be proud of what action she took?
- Do I believe I was born worthy of love and belonging? How do I practice this belief?
- Borrowed from Alexander Chee's *How to Write an Auto-biographical Novel*: Dying, what stories would I tell?

Whatever your questions, love them all. Take them into your dark woods, your deep, looping meditation.

And when you emerge, the story you carry will be yours alone.

CHAPTER 1

Confidence Is Performance

And How to Do It

I've learned to address the craft of pitching in both practical and psychological terms. The pitching templates and Q&As are coming, but first I want to start with a double portrait. Here is a snapshot of my professional life story, otherwise known as an author bio. I'll follow that snapshot by telling you more about how that biography feels inside my skin.

I've been publishing for about twenty years. I published my first poem when I was sixteen and got my first magazine staff writer position at age nineteen. I received my BA and MFA from Columbia and finished my formal education when I was twenty-four. After graduating, I got a full-time writing job in an intercultural newsroom in San Francisco, and I acquired a literary agent who helped me sell my first novel when I was twenty-five. I spent two years reporting in that newsroom and teaching writing in the Santa Clara County juvenile justice system, and I published that novel, a gay YA hip-hopera called *Sister Mischief,* in 2011.

In 2012, I raised $150,000 from Kickstarter donations and private investors to produce the independent feature film I co-wrote with my friend Meera, *Farah Goes Bang*, and that film premiered at the Tribeca Film Festival in 2013, where it won the first $25,000 Nora Ephron Prize from Tribeca and *Vogue*. I also published a collection of poems, *Become a Name*, with a small press called Fathom Books in 2016. Throughout all of this, I've published nonfiction about gender, race, culture, and media in magazines such as *BuzzFeed Reader, ELLE, New Republic, Catapult*, and *The Cut*, and that nonfiction work has garnered me fellowships from San José State University and the Bread Loaf Writers' Conference. I'm now an associate director at the Public Humanities Initiative and a lecturer in English and feminist, gender, and sexuality studies at Stanford University.

Why would I give you this bird's-eye view of my résumé? Well, you don't know me. It's incumbent on me to be able to provide you with this snapshot, because for our work together to succeed, you need assurance of my credibility as an authority on the subject of pitching and publishing. To demonstrate that credibility, I'm going to choose proper nouns you're likely to recognize: Columbia, MFA, San José State, Tribeca, Bread Loaf, Stanford. I chose this language because the way I've been educated means I already know a few things about you too: You're probably bright and interested in institutional recognition. I'm going to note that I was young when I put some of these notches on my résumé because I suspect many of the people reading this are as young and impatient as I once was. Through my diction, I can create the impression that you and I already have many things in common, building a sense of solidarity between us. Once that solidarity exists, we are in conversation with each other, and this has been my goal all along.

Confidence: It's All Performance

In essence, what I've executed with this strategic explanation of my professional history is a performance of confidence platformed on a summary of where I've accrued cultural capital—which is an extremely graduate school way of saying "author bio."

This kind of performance of confidence forms the substance of pitching itself. I argued in the Introduction that all confidence is performance, and I'll argue here that all capitalism predicates itself on what I'm calling an economy of confidence: This economy expands from a series of sales, and each sale represents a performance of confidence that is rewarded with money.

However, what my performance of confidence may also have done, erroneously, is give you the impression that, after getting my grubby little paws on multiple book deals, a film release, a bunch of individual publications, and a job I love, I've reached a point in my career where I no longer feel fear, insecurity, doubt, shame, or stress. Much to the detriment of my mental, physical, and spiritual health, I have often conflated my worth as a human being with my publications list, my GPA, the selectiveness of the schools I attended, my tax return, my job title, my weight, and what other people thought of me.

I'm bringing these discomforts to the forefront because I don't ever want you to think that anyone's "success" in the literary field, or any field, can exempt them from failure, rejection, doubt, shame, or insecurity. These are our gifts for life.

Here I'd like to offer you a quick ego-scan: Below is a series of questions that will reveal where your very human ego is probably harboring some fear, shame, anxiety, or insecurity. Consider each question individually and answer Yes or No privately to yourself.

- Does thinking about pitching an editor or agent arouse any fear or anxiety?
- Does giving someone the power to reject your work make you feel fearful or anxious?
- Does finding a larger audience for your work, especially an audience that might include your friends and family members, make you feel at all fearful or anxious?
- Have you ever felt like there's no road map for the kind of career you want?
- Be honest: Do you suspect you're probably less qualified even to be reading this book than most of the other people reading it?

If these questions stirred up any sticky feelings, I want you to know this: In every for   here I've taught this material in person, without fail, nearly every hand in the room has shot into the air at these questions. I've seen Olympians, deans, tenured professors, major award winners, and authors of multiple books raise their hands at these questions.

When we enter a learning space, it's easy to assume that we should check our fears at the door, or at least pretend they're not there. But while you read, I'd like to propose instead that you make a little space next to you, no bigger than a small chicken or a large cupcake, for your fear to sit and join our exploration. Your fear is welcome, but it's not in charge.

So how do we combat impostor syndrome? How do we slay

the demons that cause us to doubt and undermine ourselves? In addition to maintaining perspective and cultivating community, another strategy, and probably why you're reading this book, is to arm ourselves with information. What I've found in my years of studying pitching, both as a practitioner and as an instructor, is that, just as our identities and marginalities are culturally constructed, so too can the performance of confidence be constructed. There is actually a formula you can follow that builds on itself as a model of how to fake it until you make it. I've identified seven distinct and cumulative steps in performing confidence as a writer seeking work. They are as follows:

1. **GENERATE AN IDEA FOR A STORY!** You cannot pitch or write a story until a small kernel of an idea sprouts in your mind. This is a hard, crucial part of the process, and it's glib of me to write "generate an idea" as if it's easy. Here are some questions I have sometimes used to develop story ideas:

    On what subject could you walk into a bar right now and speak passionately and extemporaneously for twenty minutes? In other words, on what subject are you an expert?

    What are your guiltiest pleasures? Why are they pleasurable to you? What makes you feel guilty for enjoying them?

    What works of art (books, TV shows, films, videogames, and so on) have you read/watched/experienced more than twice? What keeps you coming back?

What story does your (or someone else's) full name tell?

Two people have a conflict. Neither of them is wrong. What happens?

You perceived something you couldn't name as a child. How would you name it now?

Most people misunderstand how a [process, place, trend, or ideology] works. How is it commonly misunderstood, and how does it really work?

2. **BELIEVE YOURSELF TO BE QUALIFIED.** This step is hard, and in my observation, it's where most people drop out of the game. It can be strategically overstepped; it is possible to send a pitch without believing yourself to be qualified. But I recommend sending pitches from the mindset that you have the ability to write the story competently, that your writing has value, and that an editor or another gatekeeper might recognize this.

3. **IDENTIFY WHO TO CONTACT ABOUT YOUR IDEA.** What kind of publication or editor might be interested in your story? This step requires reading, research, and networking, and you've probably already done more of it than you realize. Some great places to start: calls for pitches on social media, your favorite books' acknowledgments pages, and the mastheads of your favorite publications.

4. **ARGUE COGENTLY FOR YOUR IDEA.** It's not enough just to come up with an idea for a story; your pitch needs to demonstrate that you can execute on the story itself, that you've chosen its editorial target with care, and that the story will be relevant to that publication's target audience. Your project here is, in essence, to make an argument for your argument.

5. **GAUGE HOW MUCH YOUR ARGUMENT IS WORTH RELATIVE TO THE MARKET.** Your strongest points of leverage to consider here are how much time, research, and length will be necessary to execute on your pitch; how much the publication has paid other writers; and how much you've been paid in the past. My single most valuable resource in step 5 is the website whopayswriters .com, which lists rates for almost every publication on the market.

6. **ENFORCE AND MAXIMIZE THAT VALUE AFTER THE STORY IS DELIVERED.** I truly wish this aspect of the writing profession didn't require its own line item, but it's been my experience that collecting the money you're owed, that is, chasing checks, tends to occupy a lot of time and effort. The best you can do is have your paperwork at the ready and not be afraid to follow up. It's also good form to promote the story on your own social media, then to ask your editor for readership metrics on your story, which can be useful for future pitches.

7. **CULTIVATE SOLIDARITY WITH A COMMUNITY OF LIKE-MINDED WRITERS.** This sounds like a nice-to-have, but I stand to testify it's a must-have. You cannot gather information without a community, and neither can you sustain the

intrinsic self-doubt and rejection of the writing life alone. You need friends you can ask, "Hey, how was your experience working with this editor? This agent? How much did they pay you? Did you get paid on time?" You need people you trust enough to read your shitty first drafts. Karma is real: Be generous with favors and information and the same will flow back to you.

Because pitching exists within the machinations of capitalism, these seven steps constitute a marketable formula that can be executed to produce income. Information about how to navigate the system attacks impostor syndrome at its root.

So. It sounds pretty simple to break this down into seven steps, but I know, and you know, that putting yourself out there for opportunities is more complicated than that.

The Vast, Existential, Unavoidable Questions of Pitching—and Their Answers

I've taught something like thirty different pitching classes for emergent writers, and through this work I've had the opportunity to study what questions students of all different backgrounds and disciplines ask again and again, what their most common impediments to successful pitching are, and how accurately students tend to assess themselves relative to the market. I have learned that teaching a performance of confidence as emotionally and financially risky as pitching necessitates a deep engagement with the psychologies of fear and anxiety, and a counterbalancing attention to mindfulness and community.

I emphasize the *performance* of confidence because, within capitalism, the stakes of confidence have much less to do with how you *feel* than with how you *act* or *behave*. The writer who sends a well-composed email while fighting waves of nausea from behind a hand clutched over her face can still earn money via the act of writing and sending that email. As long as the point of sale is presented through the pitch's performance of confidence, the actual feelings surrounding it recede in importance.

Now that we've done a few tips and tricks, it's time to review the two biggest, scariest, most dauntingly existential questions that I hear from students in every single pitching class.

Will people be mad at me?

If my pitch is on the wrong subject or too many words or directed to the wrong editor, will its recipient be mad? If I follow up because I haven't received an answer on my pitch or a payment I'm owed, will I piss someone off? If I negotiate with an editor to ask for more money, will they be so horrified by my boldness that they rescind their offer? If I ask a contact to share another contact, will they be offended by that request? And most of all, if I do make someone mad, will their anger place me on a permanent blacklist that gatekeepers maintain behind closed doors?

When I dig deeper into the *Will people be mad at me?* question, I witness deep investment. You wouldn't care if someone was mad at you about something that means nothing to you, right? I also hear impostor syndrome in the fear of angering people: *Will people be mad at me?* simultaneously asks *Do I belong here? Will I be exposed as a fraud? Will I violate rules because I don't know what they are?*

Most everybody fears anger, and as you'll recall, we're allowing fear to remain with us, in a seat no bigger than a small chicken or a large cupcake. I would also note that anger, like fear, is an emotional attachment, and most recipients of your pitches will feel no emotional attachment to you, or those pitches, whatsoever. You are invested in and attached to your story idea, so on some level you assume that the recipient of your idea is just as invested and attached. But they aren't. This might be cold consolation, but most recipients of your pitches simply won't care enough about them to get angry at you.

Here we collide with a paradox: Because academia tends to reward people-pleasing and perfectionism, most people who excel at school tend toward people-pleasing and perfectionism. Yet confident pitching relies on a fundamental willingness to take risks and make mistakes. As long as you wouldn't be offended to receive the email you're sending, then send it. I have even sent emails that were imperfect or overreaching and still achieved their goal. I combat my own people-pleasing and perfectionism by taking a nothing-to-lose attitude: I currently have no byline at X publication. If my pitch gets rejected, I'm in the exact same position. I have nothing to lose and everything to gain just by giving it a shot. Though I am not a person naturally inclined toward sports metaphors, the maxim remains that you miss 100 percent of the shots you don't take.

When we move past *Will people be mad at me?*, we can observe how confidence actually tends to behave. In my observation of pitching praxis, confidence is the engine that empowers us to stand behind our own accomplishments rather than downplaying them; to consider ourselves qualified enough to be taken seriously by an editor or publication; to write a declarative, purposeful proposal of our idea; to collect on the money we're owed for stories or services delivered; and to use a cold pitch as an opener to building a farther-reaching relationship. Confidence values what we have already achieved and experienced expressly so that we can open ourselves to new achievements and experiences.

I must also note that *any thorough explication of confidence must account for which presentations of confidence our culture tends to reward.* All capitalist economies privilege the white, the male, the wealthy, the young, the physically and mentally able, the thin, the conventionally attractive, the childless or dependent-less, the cis, and the hetero. This is a fact, supported by myriad data. It can be so easy to forget how much of *feeling* is a cultural construction: Our culture cues us to feel and indeed behave in different ways according to our identities.

Against this backdrop, it becomes a political action for me, a queer white woman supporting two dependents, to present an argument for my value, and to assign a value to my argument, with confidence. It is a logical and understandable response to behave in the ways our culture rewards—for white mothers, for example, to strive to be likable, thin, deferent, and gentle—but it is also possible, and highly political, to deploy confidence as a tool to dissemble these toxic feedback loops.

However, here is where I must also make a big, unignorable disclaimer: I am a white woman, raised by American-born parents with Western modes of financial literacy, educated in predominantly white institutions. My performance of confidence is racialized, as well as gendered, and it would be disingenuous for me to pretend otherwise. Like all white writers, whether they admit it in print or not, my pitches and professional trajectory have directly benefited from white supremacy. There is no way I can escape that my performance of confidence and its rewards are informed by whiteness.

This book connects that uneasy knowledge to action. First, I explicitly acknowledge the likelihood, rooted in down-home American racism, that my performances of confidence will be rewarded more frequently and lucratively than will those offered by my colleagues of color. In acknowledging that ugly injustice, next, I accept that part of my workload as a white writer has to be sharing the privileges that have been unequally bestowed on me as widely and proactively as I can. I also resist centering my white performance of confidence as the only viable kind: Rather, my hope is that many people, of many identities, will adapt my principles to serve their own unique circumstances. Abiding by this ethic, in writing and publishing this book I seek to act against white supremacy and misogyny through the free and promiscuous sharing of previously gatekept information. Indeed, I believe candid information sharing to be another performance of confidence, an inherently political one, and one available to all of us.

Synthesizing these points produces one of the core values of this book: When information that affects our livelihoods, that informs the height of our ambitions, that limns the magnitude of our dreams, is restricted behind the walls of expensive graduate programs and legacy magazines, then the vibrancy of the entire writing community suffers. "Insider information" just signifies employment information that has traditionally been available only to rich, straight, cis, college-educated white men. When I metabolize that information, I expand its principles to insist upon my inclusion; when I distribute that information, we expand it together to insist upon yours. In any context, confidence can be resistance, and it contains radical potential.

Even if I can manage my fear of rejection, how do I withstand rejection itself?

To talk about professional writing is to talk about rejection. Rejection is part of every writer's job, and as you've heard, I have quite a bit of experience with it. I've only ever found two meaningful strategies to sustain myself through the disappointment of rejection.

One is to treat rejection as progress, and as information. I often say that the arc of a writer's career is predictable: First you get silence; then you get form rejections; then you get nice, personalized rejections; then finally you get an acceptance. Each step begets the next: You can't know whether your pitches are even worth responding to until someone rejects them. I've gotten some of the most actionable feedback of my career from decision-makers who were generous enough to share *why* they passed on my project. It is worth knowing when something isn't working, and even more worthwhile to know why.

Rejections are terribly subjective, sometimes arbitrary, and extremely difficult not to take personally. But they are also, at a base level, *information,* and all information is valuable to you in constructing a strategy for your next moves. If you can treat rejections more as information than as a referendum on your personal worth, rejections can benefit you.

My other strategy for withstanding rejection is building community. Have you ever noticed that writing is *terrible*? This practice is singular in its solitude: your task is to sit alone for as many hours as you can steal from your other obligations and attempt to channel your volatile, incoherent inner monologue into a legible product. This is difficult and painful work. The only colleagues you will have in this solitary labor will be the people with whom you choose to share that monologue, both before and after it exists as a product. You have to choose your own community.

Let me share a personal example. Once I asked my longtime therapist how she maintains a practice of self-care—not just getting a good night's sleep and maybe a pedicure or massage once in a while, but protecting herself daily from being completely debilitated by the force of other people's traumas. She was so ready for this question she didn't even pause in answering it. She said that she practices fifteen minutes a day of mindful meditation and meets weekly with a group of other therapists as support for her professional practice. She framed this community not as one of social indulgence or discretionary time to unwind—this was not trivia night or happy hour—but as an essential bulwark for her professional survival.

I liked this model, and about five years ago I called a fiction writer I know from grad school, told him what my therapist had said, and suggested we schedule a monthly call to reflect and support each other in our writing and publishing practices. We call these meetings our "professional wellness check-ins." These calls can take the form of dissecting the etymologies of obscure words, venting about how hard it is to write while parenting young children, or seeking each other's input on specific writing and career questions. After every call, I feel buoyed by the reminder that writing is hard, that everybody gets rejections, and that I'm not alone in the struggle of channeling my inner monologue. I cannot recommend this practice enough: Pick a reliable writer friend and schedule a regular professional wellness check-in.

If there is one thing that I hope you take from this, it is simply that you are capable of pitching and worthy of being taken seriously. This is the premise from which we begin: If you have done the work of having an idea, thoughtfully targeting who might be interested in it, and making an informed argument for that idea's quality, relevance, and deliverability, you deserve to be considered. Confidence is a cultural construct, and you are just as entitled to perform it as anybody else.

CHAPTER 2

Build Your Online Platform

Author Websites, Bios,
Social Media, and Newslettering

To convey that your work deserves to be taken seriously, make yourself findable on the internet in a way that represents you as appealingly as possible. Your online platform will best represent you if it is current, complete, and professional. Here are some of my best practices for making a great first impression with your online platform.

Any Author Website Is Better Than No Website

A basic author website is an invaluable tool for ensuring that people can find you online, identify you as a professional writer, and commission work from you. It's just a signature, a quick professional self-portrait, to make it easier for someone to dig deeper into your body of work. **I view an author website as a digital business card:** It's not as much about garnering two hundred thousand unique daily visitors as it is about making sure the right information on you is available to a few key visitors. A simple, current website that makes it easy to contact you is 500 percent more valuable than an elaborately gorgeous website that hasn't been updated in a decade. That's just math.

Your website should contain three key elements: **clips of your past work, your author bio, and your contact information.** Many authors structure this as three tabs: one page for links to your work, one page for your author bio, and one page for your contact information. For certain professionals, like academics, it may also be appropriate to include a full curriculum vitae (CV). Depending on what's most relevant to you, you can also add pages for different genres you write in, your social media channels, and your blog or newsletter. It's a *fantastic* idea to integrate a few key words about the topics that interest you most: for example, "Laura Goode writes about intersectional feminism, female relationships, motherhood, gender, and race in TV, film, culture, and literature." Once you've covered the bases of providing a brief snapshot of your work and an easy way to contact you, feel free to be creative with the rest.

WHAT ARE CLIPS?

Clips or *clippings* are terms used to describe your previously published work. The word comes from the newspaper era, when you literally had to keep a book of your articles clipped out from papers, but it still applies to links or PDFs of your stories. You can include these at the end of a pitch email, or in a short/medium author bio appended to the bottom.

Having a simple author website is so easy these days that even the most technophobic among us can pull it off. While the platforms and their proper nouns are constantly changing, a number of them will host your site for prices ranging from free to $100–$200 per year, and surfing five to ten of your favorite authors' homepages will surely give you a sense of the current options. Any of these hosts offer a ton of customized designs that make it easy to slap a serviceable site together literally in minutes.

A thematic note here: As a baseline, for reasons of simplicity, professionalism, and search engine optimization, **I recommend choosing a domain name that hews close to your publishing name,** rather than inventing a whimsical online handle, like the AOL Instant Messenger screen names I created in the early 2000s. Lauragoode.com conveys a lot more authority and legibility than porcupen.com, which is the *least* embarrassing former screen name I could have chosen for this teachable moment.

If there's ever original or photo art involved in any of your pieces, those can be great images to include on your website—link these eye-catching images to their corresponding stories. Some people also use publications' logos as images that link to their stories in those publications. If you use any original art (excluding logos), always credit the artist or photographer.

Of the elements I've just listed, "past work" tends to generate the most anxiety. It's a natural question: *What clips can I possibly list if I haven't published much, or at all?*

If you don't have a lot of bylines and clips yet, then it can be a great idea to share some of your ideas using a democratic platform such as a blog or newsletter: Tumblr, Medium, Substack, or whatever is popular when you read this. If you feel an irrepressible urge to write something, then write it by any means necessary. This kind of material can certainly help you develop your portfolio and online presence if it feels organic and desirable to you to post some sentences on one of these accessible platforms.

All of that said, please don't blog because you Just Feel Like You Should. It's my conviction that blogging is not now what it was in its early-2000s heyday—as I write this in 2024, newsletters seem to have filled that space—and your author website doesn't really need to get a ton of traffic when its primary purpose is to introduce you to people who are already interested. Moreover, writers deserve to get paid, which blogging does not usually achieve. So write a blog or newsletter if it feels right to you, but if it doesn't, find another medium to update regularly that suits you better.

Another very common source of author-website anxiety emerges in questions such as this: *How do I make myself extremely findable to all the people who might be impressed by, supportive of, and inclined to pay for my writing, while also remaining 100 percent incognito to my parents, enemies, exes, app dates, and day job circle because the thought of them reading my innermost thoughts on the internet makes me dry-heave?*

Well, this is a two-parter.

Part one: While there is no foolproof way to control who reads your innermost thoughts after you've published them, a pseudonym can sometimes be worth considering. Certain writers, particularly nonfiction writers, have high-stakes safety and security concerns in publishing, which I would like to separate from the general fear of exposure that almost all of us feel. If the subject matter of your writing causes you to fear retribution from any person or entity—say, a violent ex, a toxic family or community of origin, an information-sensitive job—with the potential to harm you physically, emotionally, financially, or legally, then a pseudonym can provide an important measure of self-protection. If you're in this kind of situation, I'm so sorry; I commend your courage in writing about it, and I also recommend seeking support from allies such as lawyers and therapists as you navigate publishing.

Part two: And then there are the rest of us, who are just terrified for myriad, ambient reasons. This is so understandable; writing is self-exposure! It's nauseating and thrilling at the same time, and I've found that the feelings of exposure get easier to handle with practice. For us Regular Afraids, the option of using a pseudonym is still available, and if you're concerned about professional boundaries between creative work and "day job" work, many people choose to make two websites, or different pages on the same website, for each.

But past that, you do have to decide whether you're going to make yourself and your work findable or not. The truth in an internet age is that every time you decide to publish something under your given name, you are adding to the store of what can be found by googling you: Once you're findable, you're findable. That said, in my experience, people will judge your innermost thoughts much less negatively than your inner critic would imagine.

Writing Your Author Bio to Minimize Shame and Maximize Shine

How we describe our work begins with how we describe ourselves. A thoughtful author biography makes you appear polished, professional, and prepared for conversations about your work. Different people, inquiries, and situations will call for different bios—with each piece of correspondence, you want to use your bio to highlight the parts of your work that seem most relevant to the person you're contacting. What do you have in common with them? Did you grow up in the same area or attend the same school? Have you published an article that's similar in length, tone, tense, or topic to the one you're pitching? Are they always tweeting about a TV show you're obsessed with and want to cover? If you can't locate any obvious common ground, simply highlight what you think is your strongest work. A bio is nothing more than an opportunity for a reader to learn a little more about you, your experience, and your interests.

In your bio, include whatever feels most relevant or impressive of the following: **publications, awards, alma maters, degrees, jobs, projects you're currently developing, and/or links to your work, website, newsletter, blog, or social media channels.** Proceed backward chronologically, beginning with your most recent work and ending with the oldest, as you would with a résumé or CV. Similarly, begin with what you think is most impressive— either in terms of the publication or the quality of your work—and proceed into the less recognizable from there. Most people write bios in the third person, even though this feels a little strange while you're writing. Do your best to use active, interesting language and, obviously, provide only truthful and verifiable information. **Being dishonest is far worse than being inexperienced.**

If you need to trim a bio for length, start by cutting the oldest and most obscure items. A hobbyhorse of mine: Don't describe yourself as "award-winning" unless the award is significant enough to mention by name, in which case it's more impressive to specify "Pushcart Prize–winning" anyway. Try not to include links that direct people *away* from your work; the principle of bio linking is to provide just enough links (to your own writing) to whet readers' appetite for your body of work, but not so many that they get totally distracted or lost down an internet rabbit hole.

Reasonable people disagree with me here, but it's my opinion that since the bio is primarily a showcase for your work experience, not your relationships, it's not a place for extensive descriptions of spouses/partners, children, or pets. The most obvious exception to this recommendation is if your book directly addresses one of these personal relationships—if your book is a memoir about the struggle to find a diagnosis for your son's mysterious illness, like my friend Taylor Harris's gorgeous memoir *This Boy We Made,* then it makes sense to include a mention of your family in the book's author bio, as Taylor did.

Separately from this exception, please allow me a brief sermon on this subject. As a woman, I've noticed that women tend to mention personal relationships in bios much more often than men do—which makes complete sense, given that women in our culture are trained from birth to locate their value in relationship to others. (Men list these personal relationships in the acknowledgments page, where they reveal that their wives did all the research, typing, editing, and other unpaid labor that went into the book.) I'm probably making this recommendation because I'm tired of reading Wikipedia pages about brilliantly accomplished women that deliver eight paragraphs on their romantic lives and one sentence about their eight published books, and tired of attending author Q&As where the first question is "What did your husband/child/mother think of this book?" I'm extremely tired of not being able to control the rampant misogyny in the world. But I know that my author bio is a depiction of my professional experience that I *can* control.

Your author bio is a showcase for your work. Showcase it with pride.

Short, Medium, and Long Author Bios

For all styles of self or story synopses—bios, project descriptions, and so on—I recommend having short, medium, and long versions on hand. I qualify a "short" author bio as one or two lines, a "medium" bio as a brief paragraph, and a "long" bio as about one page. Most of the time, a pitch, query, application, or other professional correspondence calls for a short- to medium-length author bio. I'll often append my medium bio to a cold-pitch email; editors will usually use the short version with the published story. I generally use the long version only on my website or with a big submission: my agent sending a book out to editors, a prestigious fellowship application, and the like.

In a bio of any length, don't be vague just to fill space. I'm reminded of a bio that said, "Ralph is waiting to see what is next in life." Aren't we all? The authors with the most name recognition tend to have the shortest bios, so it can be a power move to keep it brief. "Zadie Smith lives in London" conveys "You *know* who the fuck I am."

MY SHORT, MEDIUM, AND LONG BIOS

SHORT: Laura Goode is the author of two books: the young adult novel *Sister Mischief* (Candlewick Press, 2011) and the collection of poems *Become a Name* (Fathom Books, 2016). She lives in San Francisco.

MEDIUM: Laura Goode is the author of a collection of poems, *Become a Name* (Fathom Books, 2016), and a novel for young adults, *Sister Mischief* (Candlewick Press, 2011), which was a 2012 Best of the Bay pick by the *San Francisco Bay Guardian* and a selection of two ALA honor lists. She wrote (with director Meera Menon) and produced the feature film *Farah Goes Bang,* which premiered at the 2013 Tribeca Film Festival and won the inaugural Nora Ephron Prize from Tribeca and *Vogue.* Her nonfiction has appeared in *BuzzFeed, New York Maga-*

zine, Longreads, ELLE, Catapult, Refinery29, and elsewhere. She received her BA and MFA from Columbia University and lives in San Francisco.

LONG: Laura Goode writes about intersectional feminism, female friendship, motherhood, gender, and race in culture, TV, film, and literature.

Her collection of poems, *Become a Name,* was released by Fathom Books in October 2016. "This collection," wrote the poet Harmony Holiday, "possesses the fugitive elegance of all well-behaved rebels who know how to breach the pattern from within it, who rename themselves again and again, against the myth of finitude."

Her feature film, *Farah Goes Bang,* premiered at the Tribeca Film Festival in April 2013, where it won the inaugural Nora Ephron Prize from Tribeca and *Vogue.* She co-wrote the film with director Meera Menon and produced it. *Farah Goes Bang* follows three recent college graduates who go on the road in 2004 to campaign for John Kerry and get laid. It raised $81,160 on Kickstarter in 2012. During its run at eighteen other national and international film festivals, it was honored with three Best Narrative Feature awards, among other accolades. *Farah Goes Bang* was released on iTunes, Amazon, Google Play, Vimeo, and Seed&Spark in April 2015.

Her novel for young adults, *Sister Mischief,* was released by Candlewick Press on July 12, 2011. Elissa Schappell wrote of *Sister Mischief* in *Vanity Fair*'s Hot Type, "You can't help but cheer as Goode's crew—starring Esme, a Jewish lesbian songwriter who goes by 'M. C. Ferocious'; D. J. SheStorm, a badass breeder; and M. C. Rohini, a hot desi chick and Ferocious's love interest—take over a pep rally, read Diane di Prima, and throw down rhymes." The American Library Association included *Sister Mischief* in two of its annual honor lists: the Amelia Bloomer Project, recognizing excellence in feminist YA literature, and the Rainbow List (Top Ten selection), recognizing excellence in

GLBTQ YA. *Sister Mischief* was also a 2012 Best of the Bay pick by the *San Francisco Bay Guardian.*

Her nonfiction has appeared widely in *BuzzFeed, Catapult, Glamour, InStyle, Longreads, The Cut, Refinery29, New Republic,* and many other publications. Her cross-genre work has also appeared in anthologies including *Starry Eyed: 16 Stories That Steal the Spotlight, Please Excuse This Poem: 100 New Poets for the Next Generation,* and *Scratch: Writers, Money, and the Art of Making a Living.* That nonfiction has received support from the 2018–2019 Steinbeck Fellowship at San José State University and the 2019 Bread Loaf Writers' Conference.

Goode was raised in Edina, Minnesota; received her BA in English and comparative literature and her MFA in writing from Columbia University; and now teaches at Stanford University.

For authors writing bios in more emergent stages of a career, have no fear. Anyone can write an engaging bio that includes (a) interesting jobs you've held, (b) fun facts about yourself, (c) where you live, or (d) what you're working on. "Laura Goode has been a nursing home waitress, a New York City bartender, a spelling bee champion, and a prison writing teacher, and she once placed second runner-up in the Miss Preteen Minneapolis personality pageant. She lives in San Francisco and at lauragoode.com." Remember: A brief bio conveys confidence.

A few final notes on what to consider including in author websites and bios: If you've done artistic work in another discipline, and this work feels in any way relevant to the writing interests you wish to showcase, then including this kind of professional history can help to illuminate who you are. Work that isn't directly related to writing can often serve to add some interesting personality and dimensionality to you as a human being.

Many writers work in ghostwriting, copywriting, copyediting, or other uncredited forms of language generation, and this is impressive enough to mention; it shows you write clean copy with strong grammar, deliver on deadline, and collaborate well with others. If you'd like to reference this kind of experience, you can (a) include links to stories you've ghostwritten if that's permissible under whatever agreement you made with the person/company you've ghosted for, or (b) include a bio line or two such as "Zendaya has also ghostwritten two biographies for prominent business leaders."

For clips that aren't available online, link to PDFs (host them on your website) of print stories, if possible. If you're still able to contact the publication, do so with permission.

To protect your intellectual property, I discourage extensive excerpts or descriptions of unpublished work in a bio or website, but it's fine to mention something short and tantalizing like "Balthazar is at work on a novel/memoir about XYZ."

Building Your Social Media Presence

Social media is a sprawling and controversial subject in our dystopian contemporary era; entire books dissect this subject, but this isn't one of them. My general social media advice is that if you intend to make your writing public—which is not a requirement, but I'm assuming that if you bought this book, you do—you will probably benefit from having an active profile on at least one of the following: TikTok, LinkedIn, Instagram, X/Twitter, Substack (or another newslettering platform), or Medium. These companies and proper nouns turn over quickly, so the principle to remember is to make yourself findable in one or two places. This may be the only time I choose a military analogy, but the U.S. Army uses an acronym, PACE, to describe the importance of maintaining multiple lines of communication—Primary, Alternate, Contingency, Emergency—and this provides a useful lens through which to view the constantly shifting ground of digital communication.

I think writers tend to shine on text-based platforms; X/Twitter attracted writers for a long time on this basis. Whether the most appealing text-based platform by the time you read this is X/Twitter, Bluesky, or another proper noun I don't know yet, these are forums where you can "meet" and respond to people you don't know IRL, so they're good places for sharing and engagement. Text-based platforms are great places for pitching intel: I see editors posting calls for pitches, preferences about what they're looking for, and job notices. I see writers crediting their editors and agents. I see writers forming friendships and professional alliances.

None of this is to elide that the infinite scroll can also be a churning cesspool of rage bait, harassment, and bad faith. I encourage you to block, mute, and unfollow promiscuously when you encounter these bad takes and bad actors. A social media presence is never worth sacrificing your sanity or humanity, and I observe people I know who have large (read: overwhelming) followings taking frequent breaks from the platform.

Nonetheless, as in almost all things, I have found on social media that—with a few irrational exceptions—I've reaped what I sow. I make an active commitment with my social media presence that even though I swear like a barmaid, I don't snark, I don't punch down, and I keep 98 percent of my contributions to the conversation warm and supportive. On the rare occasions that I get in a flame war, it's almost always because I've witnessed someone else making what my six-year-old son would call "sad choices." (For example, I have a *lot* of choice words for professors who tweet student work to make fun of it.)

You can follow me at lauragoode.substack.com on Substack or @thereallauragoode on Instagram, but part of me hopes you don't, because my life with fewer than five thousand followers is still relatively peaceful.

In all phases of marketing, writers routinely panic about not having a large enough social media following. If you want to increase that following, you have three options:

- Engage a lot, consistently and organically, over a long period of time; follow interesting people; occasionally muster the courage to add something to the conversation; and share stuff you like,
- Go randomly viral on a story or tweet, or
- Buy Russian bots. (Strongly discouraged; glory to Ukraine.)

Another deeply common area of struggle is balancing the need to maintain a social media presence while avoiding extreme procrastination on writing. Time management is incredibly personal, but I do have a few tips.

I find, most of all, that the first pages I open when I sit down to work will set the precedent for that day's concentration and work ethic. If I start out by opening the document of the piece I'm working on, I'm much likelier to stay engaged with it than if I start the day idly scrolling.

Some people find apps or browser extensions that block certain distracting sites for blocks of writing time really helpful. I'm not a religious user of these but have sometimes found StayFocusd useful.

The flexibility of my teaching schedule is a privilege I must acknowledge here, but I have always tried to organize the hours of my day with writing at the fore. My best writing hours tend to be in the morning, so I try to preserve 8 a.m. to noon for just writing, and then I try to save meetings, errands, or emails for the afternoon. Of course, I violate my own principles all the time, but it helps to keep the general priority structure in mind. Do your utmost to protect the time of day when you write best.

I also find that if I'm in a demanding stretch of writing, I do best if I take structured breaks, like two hours of writing, then ten to fifteen minutes of social media.

On the subject of time management, Melissa Febos's canonical essay for *Catapult*, "Do You Want to Be Known for Your Writing, or for Your Swift Email Responses?," offers another pro tip:

> I schedule writing time on my calendar. This is a good practice. The problem was that for many years I had no respect for those appointments. A friend or colleague would ask a favor or invite me to lunch (Lunches: They ruin perfectly good days of writing), and I would stand up my work without hesitation. If I bailed on any friend as often as I bailed on my own work, I probably would no longer have that friend.
>
> Then, one day, someone asked a favor during a time I had saved for writing and I said that I had an appointment. This was technically true, but in my mind I pretended that it was a doctor's appointment. And it worked; I wrote that day.

Launching a Newsletter

I strongly recommend having a newsletter. I started a newsletter on TinyLetter—Ovaries and Bovaries: The Hell of a Dame—in 2015, then transitioned it to become Re/Definitions on Substack after TinyLetter shuttered in 2024.

Why do I feel so strongly about the efficacy of newsletters? I have multiple times as many X/Twitter followers as I do newsletter subscribers—but newsletters get a dramatically greater engagement than tweets. Every newsletter I send has an average 65 percent open rate. My last newsletter was opened by 74 percent of my subscribers. So if I want something to get read, I'm going to drop it in the inbox. Social media is a volatile bet; the inbox is somewhat more consistent.

I see newslettering as an opportunity to broaden and deepen a loyal readership/audience for your future stories and especially for when you want to sell books or promote events in the future. A newsletter mailing list is like an ideal bank account: It grows with time, earning interest. You're not just building your newsletter for the work you want to promote now; you're investing gradually, one email address at a time, in a go-to list for the work you'll want to promote six months, one year, and five years from now.

So, even if you're not sure you have much to say or promote now, even if you just slap together a list of say, fifty to one hundred friends and family members—there it is, ready to go when you land a byline in a dream publication eight months from now. And say you send around that dream byline in eight months, and everyone loves it, then maybe ten of your subscribers forward it to their friends and you get ten more subscribers. Or you're savvy enough to include your newsletter subscription link at the end of the skillfully crafted author bio that appears with your dream byline, and you get twenty subscribers out of that. Lather, rinse, repeat, and when you want to promote a bigger project *literally years* from now, your promotion setup is locked, loaded, and loyal.

It's not important that your newsletter is especially long, or frequent, or even that you have tons of new, published pieces of work to promote in it. **It is important that you keep sending and adding subscribers to it over time.** Sending a letter even just once every two months will build your subscriber base over the course of a year. Ditto adding one new subscriber a week. You can boost new subscriptions by occasionally mentioning your newsletter in a post, including your subscription link in your social media bio, or giving away free things to your subscribers—I'll sometimes mail a free book to someone who gets five friends to subscribe. Give people something that they look forward to, and your audience will grow organically over time.

In terms of where to host newsletters, many writers use Substack, Buttondown, or Mailchimp. These offer accessible tools for adding subscribers, tracking when and how often subscribers read your letters, and embedding links, pictures, GIFs, and videos. Currently popular platforms such as Substack cost nothing for authors to use and offer options for both free releases and paid reader subscriptions: As with other constantly evolving platforms, observe what the people you admire are using, and opt for whatever seems most sustainable to your specific concerns.

On the subject of building a subscriber base, let me start with the letter of the law: It is technically illegal to subscribe people to a newsletter without their permission, and every email you send must include a visible, viable "unsubscribe" option.

That said, when you're just starting, I think there's very little risk to subscribing people in your life who support your work. The ethics of this are probably in a gray area—I'm an ask-forgiveness-not-permission kind of person, sometimes to my benefit and sometimes to my detriment. I don't think you should sign up people you don't know, or literally everyone you know, but I started my newsletter by subscribing 250–300 people who had already donated to a crowdfunding campaign I'd run, and I felt pretty secure signing up friends and acquaintances who had previously demonstrated support for my work.

Some newsletters have themes. A great way to stir up some material for your newsletter is to try logging your media diet for a week: Keep a linked list of all the stories you read in a single week. This practice has helped me notice the trends of what I like to read and makes it easier to go back and rediscover things later. It's also a good way to notice which writers, and not even necessarily famous ones, produce work you consistently love. If this accrues into a roundup that you could imagine sharing in an email, then that's a great place to start. Journalist, author, podcaster, and feminist Ann Friedman, the reigning queen of newslettering, built her email empire on nothing more than sending out well-curated links to writing she liked every Friday.

I've also seen project-based newsletters: An author sends them out for thirty days, or a summer, or the length of another project, or whatever. If that model appeals to you, I recommend checking out the archives or book version of Jami Attenberg's #1000wordsofsummer. It's a great newsletter that also transformed my whole writing practice.

Newsletters don't need mandatory, inflexible, or restrictive themes, but they can be a modular venue for your continuity of vision. What are the subjects or areas of interest you find yourself obsessing over? What is the discussion you wish people were having, and what do you have to say about it? What are you an expert on? (These questions can also be applied to pitching!) If there's something you're writing that's hard to publish in traditional media, the idea of a public-facing notebook can be appealing.

Keep your expectations manageable around how often you send out your newsletter: Once a week may not sound like much at first, but the work can pile up fast. I send mine about once a month; others send them weekly, or biweekly. I think any kind of semiregular interval is fine. You're likelier to lose subscribers by sending your newsletter too often than by not sending it often enough. I've also found that most newsletters (or new projects, generally) take time to find their tone and footing. I don't think I hit any sort of signature style for my newsletter for at least a few months.

I've sent my newsletter out at various times of day and have found that **weekday mornings tend to work best for open rates.** I haven't noticed an appreciable difference between open rates on different weekdays, but the end of the week seems to be when people are looking for things to click on when they're bored at work.

NEWSLETTERS: THE FINAL WORDS

Q: Where do I list my newsletter subscriber link?
A: I link to mine on my website, occasionally on social media, and often in my author bio.

Q: Should I allow notifications to alert me every time someone unsubscribes?
A: Absolutely not. Love yourself some.

Q: I hate self-promotion. How do I share my work?
A: Very few people *love* self-promotion, and most of them are sociopaths. The rest of us just learn to manage it as a necessary evil.

ASSIGNMENT

To close out this chapter, I'm going to give you an assignment to play with on your own time. Yes, it is extremely sassy of me to offer you assignments. I will note only two things: First, with this book as with all things, the more you put into this practice, the more you'll get out of it. Second, in my years of teaching this material, the techniques offered here have helped my students publish literally hundreds of stories, including many, many first-time publications. You might as well give it a shot, right?

- Create—or update—your personal author website. Find a host that's free/cheap and get your domain name set up.
- Write or update your short, medium, and long author bios, and put the medium or long version on your website.
- Create your newsletter on any hosting service and sign up at least twenty to thirty people who you're confident would like to receive it. Put your subscriber link on your website, author bio, or, if you're feeling brave, email signature.

CHAPTER 3

Don't Pitch Hard, Pitch Smart

The Art of Strategic Stalking . . . I Mean, Networking

Now that we've talked about making yourself findable on the internet in a way that looks professional and well curated, it's time to talk about finding others! This chapter will focus on how to find and research strategic contacts, taking us right up to the point of actually writing and sending a pitch or query, which we'll dive into over the next several chapters.

Research Always Comes First

Never, ever pitch anything to anyone without researching them first. Following are some notes on strategy, best practices, and etiquette when it comes to researching and networking with people who might be interested in your work.

A **literary agent** is someone who represents and negotiates your book deals for you. An **editor** can be (a) a person employed by a publishing house who acquires and edits books, or (b) a person employed by a newspaper, magazine, or website who acquires and edits short-form pieces.

For the purposes of this chapter's discussion, when I refer to an editor, I usually mean people in category B, who acquire and edit short-form work. Except in very select cases, authors do not pitch a long-form work (novel, memoir, essay/short story collection) directly to an editor at a publishing house; you find an agent, and then that agent pitches to editors for you. So when I talk about "pitching editors," I'm talking about pitching short-form pieces only.

It should go without saying, but probably doesn't in legal terms, that when I lightheartedly refer to "stalking" someone or acting like a "stalker," I am only referring with humor to digging up public information about a professional contact that can be readily found online, through search engines, social media, mutual contacts, or any other reasonable, public, consensual methods. In no way am I suggesting that you smack the nuclear button in the name of "research" and show up at someone's house, hack or dox them, or in any way contact them inappropriately or attempt to gain information about them that they haven't willingly shared about themselves. You should be able to obtain plenty of information about a person's interests and work history just by searching their name and visiting their website and social media channels.

A developed pitch target is a triangulation of information. On one side of the triangle, I have my own work and aspirations: the published work that demonstrates my interests and track record, the unfinished or unhoused work in my drawer, and the half-formed ideas I've been contemplating. On the second side, I have my network: the people I know who work in creative industries, who I keep up with via direct communication and social media. On the third side, I have external information: pitch calls, application rounds, and other interesting intel that I usually absorb through social media. I tend to generate pitches when I can connect at least two sides of this triangle, and when I can connect all three, that pitch is going out today.

To break this down a little further, I'll be likely to pitch an editor when I see them put out a call for pitches on social media, consistently love the stories they share, know them from another context (school, a conference), or hear about a good experience with said editor from a friend. Sometimes I'll start my research on an editor with the publication they work for, but usually I'll start with another external data point that leads me to the individual editor in particular, like a friend's story or an aptly themed upcoming issue. Once you have a general sense of what an editor's interests are, and a way to contact them, you're in a strong pitching position. Look for editors' personal websites, social media channels, LinkedIn pages, and previous work.

If you're starting with a publication rather than an editor and trying to figure out which editor is the best target for your pitch, see if the publication offers any sort of general submission guidelines—this is usually in a tab of its own at the top or bottom of the publication's landing page, or embedded in an About Us or Contact Us page. Even if you bypass the general submissions @publication.com email to contact a specific editor, follow the publication's submission guidelines: Does the publication consider unsolicited submissions only during a certain time of year? Do they consider only reported pieces? Is there a 1,600-word limit for the essays they publish in this section?

If possible, go to the publication's masthead to see their whole editorial staff and, often, their email addresses or social media handles. When you look at a masthead, see if you recognize any names. If you know someone personally, start there; if not, do some strategic stalking. Do you know someone who knows one of the editors in question, or know someone who knows someone who knows one of them? If you can dig up any degree of connection, try to e-intro your way to someone directly. But if you can't find a connection, choose the editor on the basis of who you think is likeliest to share your interests.

To do this, find them online: Many editors express submission preferences in their posts or social media bios, and many agents do the same on their websites. Furthermore, most editors and agents will promote work they've edited, as well as work they've written, on social media, so it's usually easy to see what other writers they've worked with. Do they have a personal website? What past work of theirs can you read on their personal website or on the publication where they work? From what they talk about on social media, what they've written about in the past, and who else they've published, you should be able to get a pretty good sense of what a specific contact is interested in without more than ten clicks.

If you have a personal connection to any editor, even if they're higher-level, start your pitch research there. Editors in chief (EICs) are generally not the ideal targets unless you know them or they solicit you. Usually section editors or *sometimes* managing editors (but definitely not executive/founding editors or EICs) are the ones fielding unsolicited pitches. So try to aim your pitch at the most relevant section editor, or better yet, again, e-intro your way to a connection to that editor. If a publication is cagey about their editorial contact info, they probably solicit most of their work.

A **slush pile** is where you *don't* want to go when you pitch something—it's the least specific receptacle where pitches go, like a general submissions@thiscompany.com address. Submissions to this receptacle are usually read only by an intern, and rarely do ideas make it out of slush into publication. Occasionally you hear a lightning-in-a-bottle story of a viral story or bestseller that came out of the slush pile, but these become news items because they almost never happen. (An aside: If you intend to be a professional writer, hold a job at some point where you're tasked with reading the slush pile. That this work is unsolicited does not mean it's bad, and reading it will offer you a mountain of education about what gets published and why.)

There is an unwritten rule at play here: You are allowed to bypass these info@ email addresses if you do effective research and networking. If you do the work of figuring out which editor is likeliest to be interested in your story, and you follow any guidelines they personally specify—some editors, for example, list pitching preferences on their websites or social media bios—then I do not think it's rude to send a polished pitch that makes a clear argument for why you've selected this editor. Bypassing the slush pile is absolutely the name of the game here.

Also, *ask around.* If you have a friend, acquaintance, classmate, former colleague, or other contact who's written for an interesting editor, then ask them to connect you. As long as you'd be happy to reciprocate the favor and say so, this is common practice. Getting them to pass on the desired email address to you is great; getting them to tee up an e-introduction to the desired person, thus vouching for you, is even better.

WHAT IF I CAN'T FIND SOMEONE'S EMAIL ADDRESS ONLINE?

- Ask someone else to connect you—do you know anyone, in life or on the internet, who knows or has worked with this person?
- This may sound improbable, but search their name in your own inbox—you'd be shocked at how many times I've

discovered I already had someone's email address from a group email eight years ago.

- See if you can find any email addresses of someone else who works at the same company. Usually, business email addresses follow the same structure: If John Proctor is john.proctor@salemwitch.org, then chances are that Abigail Williams is abigail.williams@salemwitch.org. Here are a few address formats for big media companies:

Bauer	firstinitiallastname@bauerpublishing.com
Condé Nast	firstname_lastname@condenast.com
Hachette	firstinitiallastname@hfmus.com
Hearst	firstinitiallastname@hearst.com
Meredith	firstname.lastname@meredith.com
Rodale	firstname.lastname@rodale.com
Reader's Digest	firstname_lastname@readersdigest.com
Time Inc	firstname_lastname@timeinc.com

If all else fails, take a shot at abigailwilliams@gmail.com or awilliams@gmail.com. A story for you: One time my friend Meera and I were in pursuit of a Pretty Famous Actress (PFA was on *SNL*) to star in the movie we were making. We tried and failed to reach her through her agent, her manager, and every other connection we could dig up on social media, alumni networks, all of it. Eventually we accepted that she wasn't interested, cast an equally incredible but less famous actress, and made the movie. Two years later, we were at a fancy women-in-Hollywood party for said movie, and lo and behold, across the room, we saw the PFA. We screwed up our courage and went over to introduce ourselves.

When PFA heard our names and the name of our movie, she screamed in our faces, grabbed our hands, and said, "Why the fuck didn't you cast me in that movie? I've been hearing about it for months!" We explained how very badly we'd wanted to cast her, and all the ways we'd tried to contact her.

She groaned, said she'd just fired her agent, and said, "You should have just emailed me. My email is firstinitiallastname @gmail.com." Lesson learned.

Best Practices for Contacting Editors

In 99.9 percent of pitching scenarios, you will be contacting an editor by email. Unless they specifically ask for submissions by postal mail, which is rare in our digital age, do not ever contact editors by phone or postal mail.

Similarly, do not attempt to pitch them on social media. Unless an editor/agent specifically says, "Tweet me your pitch using this hashtag!" or "My DMs are open for pitches for this themed issue!," I do not recommend trying to pitch via tweet, DM, Facebook message, or any other manner of social media. The social media inboxes of influential people are usually hot messes—you're very unlikely to be read, let alone responded to, there.

Do not include attachments in an initial pitch email; everything should be contained in the body of the email. Many people won't open attachments from unknown senders.

If a publication doesn't explicitly state that they do not take unsolicited pitches, usually you can take a swing at cold-pitching them. I've pitched places that say they don't take unsolicited pitches, or say they take only full stories, and gotten acceptances. I've also pitched and been told that the publication is solicitation-only: Okay, good to know. Keep in mind that publications sometimes state "rules" they don't fully mean (no unsolicited pitches, full stories only) to weed out inexperienced writers. **In any scenario, the worst any publication can do is reject you.** If Dream Publication X says they don't take unsolicited pitches and then reject you, you've lost nothing, because you already didn't have a piece published there. But if they accept your pitch, you have everything to gain.

To find out which publications pay and how much, I ask friends (and, reciprocally, share this information when asked) and consult whopayswriters.com.

In terms of the size and stature of publications you're pitching, I recommend starting smaller and working your way up. It's great to be pitching places at different levels of celebrity, but most people find the higher-value places get more attainable once a few dues have been paid. There are many "smaller" venues committed to publishing emerging writers that are reputable and put out great work, and I do think there's some worth to placing a handful of solid stories (say three to five) in nonpaying publications early in your career.

As you circle a specific publication for a pitch, read their recent archives to make sure they haven't published another piece too much like yours in the last year or so. But depending on the breadth of your subject, your task is not to ensure that they've *never* covered it before. You just have to produce a fresh and unique take on it.

In his essay collection *How to Write an Autobiographical Novel,* Alexander Chee writes about being taught by Annie Dillard:

> The literary essay, as she saw it, was a moral exercise that involved direct engagement with the unknown, whether it was a foreign civilization or your mind, and what mattered in this was you.
>
> You are the only one of you, she said. Your unique perspective, at this time, in our age, whether it's on Tunis

or the trees outside your window, is what matters. Don't worry about being original, she said dismissively. Yes, everything's been written, but also, the thing you want to write, before you wrote it, was impossible to write. Otherwise it would already exist. Your writing it makes it possible.

It is my firm conviction that **one of the best things you can do for your career—especially in its early chapters—is to do favors for and issue compliments to other people.** The publishing world is shamelessly nepotistic; relationships matter. Responding to requests for help is an easy way to build your network and cultivate relationships—recommendations, endorsements, shout-outs, likes, faves, and crowdfunding donations really do mean something, especially when you're feeling vulnerable about having just put something out into the world. People remember those small gestures. If you want audience and allies, then be the kind of person others can count on for support when they need it most.

Unsolicited shout-outs are also always welcome: **I have never met a single author who is too busy or advanced in her career to be moved by a genuine compliment on her work.** If you love a piece of work, write to the author that you love it or tell everyone you know about it—tweet about it, post about it, link to it in your newsletter. It can be a satisfying exercise as both a writer and a person to articulate exactly how much and *why* you love a piece of art, as well as a savvy way to build goodwill.

ABIDING DOS AND DON'TS
FOR CONTACTING LITERARY STRANGERS

DO be very specific and get to the main point of your email in the first paragraph. "I'd love to request an interview . . ." "I loved your book so much I had to write to tell you . . ." "With regard to the call for pitches about X that you recently tweeted, I wanted to pitch you a first-person essay about . . ." "I noticed this author lives in my area and wondered if she might be interested in giving a reading for my university's visiting-author series . . ."

DO NOT EVER email anyone you don't know asking to "pick their brain." This is a red flag to busy people that you haven't done enough homework to know what information you really want to request from them. The easier your ask is to deliver, the likelier it is to be delivered upon.

Similarly, DO NOT send an email asking for information you could have googled, and especially not to an editor. Sometimes you'll find yourself in a position of needing more information—you want to double-check that this editor is the right target at the publication, you want to know if they're open to pitches on a certain topic—and I think it's fine to ask these questions, but only if you've exhausted other modes of research.

DO demonstrate that you've done the background research I've covered in this chapter. How did you find this contact, and what in their past work indicates to you that they might be interested in yours?

DON'T expect an immediate response. DO pad in plenty of turnaround time to any pitch or request, and DO include any relevant timing information with your request. "As X's book comes out on February 10, I'd love to see the interview run within a week or two of that date."

DON'T ask anyone you don't know to read or give you general feedback on your unpublished work. It's totally reasonable to want feedback on your unpublished work—ask a friend and offer to read something for them in return. There are fewer than five people in my life for whom I would read unpublished work for free, and all of them would be just as happy to read something of mine.

DO be very reliably reciprocal about sharing contacts and doing favors: If I ask someone to share an editorial contact or other sensitive information with me, I always end the email with some version of "I hope you know I'm always happy to return a favor!" If I get a request for help from someone who's helped me in the past, I make it a priority to respond quickly and helpfully.

DO request a double-opt-in for any e-introductions you initiate. This just means approaching both individuals privately, *before* connecting them, to ask for permission to share their contact information.

Finally, DO leave your house to meet other literary folks in real life. In our internet era, I say from personal experience that it can be very tempting never to leave the house. Resist this temptation. Look for bookstores, libraries, college campuses, community centers, and other cultural gathering places in your area—get your hands on some event calendars and attend readings, lectures, performances, or other events. Bring business cards and introduce yourself to people. Ask thoughtful, craft-based questions during the Q&A. DO NOT offer thoughts during the Q&A that are more comments than questions. Buy the book, have it signed, and say hello to the author—briefly, respectfully, without trying to engage them in a long conversation as the line grows behind you. (If you have more to say than can be contained in a thirty-second exchange, write a letter.) Even though much of our lives take place online now, going places in person is still a uniquely valuable way to broaden your network, and also not a bad way to befriend other word nerds.

The $64,000 (or More) Networking Question: Should I Get a Master of Fine Arts Degree?

With regard to connection making, one of the most frequent questions I get as a writing professor is "Should I get an MFA?"

This question, like the others, varies in form. What is the specific value of an MFA? Will agents sign someone with no MFA? Do writers need an MFA in order to have a career? Where should I apply to MFA programs? And the real kicker: Do you, Laura, think your MFA was worth it?

If I had to boil my complex feelings about that last iteration of the question into a binary answer, I would almost certainly say yes, I think my MFA was worth it, to the extent that I think it was a worthwhile way to spend two years of my life. I had a wonderful experience with my program; overall my professors were phenomenal, I met brilliant friends whom I still hold very dear, and it transformed my self-conception to put writing at the forefront of my priorities, time, and life. I do earnestly feel like I grew as a writer—and as a reader, a critic, and a good art friend—as a result of that immersion.

You can already tell I'm winding up to a "but," but I'll detail all the positive aspects of the experience first.

While I definitely do *not* think every writer must obtain an MFA in order to obtain a literary agent, the most apparent return that the MFA delivered me on my investment was my first agent. The agent was someone I had known from my undergraduate years, but my doing the MFA signaled to him that I was serious about a writing career and kept me in the orbit of other writer friends he was signing. I signed with that agent right around the time of my MFA graduation, wrote the book proposal that became my first novel over the summer, and sold it in the fall. There was a lot that I didn't know then, but I'm certain that there would have been even more had it not been for my MFA education—without it, I probably wouldn't have known what a literary agent was, or why I needed one.

Another value of the program was preparing me to teach. This preparation wasn't always—indeed was almost never—expressed through hands-on teacher training, but it was conveyed through the social energy of seeing what teaching writers' lives looked like. For the professors who clearly enjoyed teaching, I could see how the classroom levied a healthy counterforce of human contact against the solitude of writing. I could see that teaching was a demanding job, but I could also see that it offered a measure of flexibility that was more or less compatible, for those who could manage their time cannily, with continuing to write. I also understood that, at the time—I got my degree at a time when very few schools offered a PhD in creative writing—the MFA was considered the terminal degree in my field, and that the degree would act as a teaching credential.

My MFA program also did an excellent job teaching me how to issue and receive feedback. Let me pause here because I still see people mess this up all the time.

HOW TO GIVE RECEIVABLE FEEDBACK

Feedback in a writing workshop, or in any forum where humanistic critique is being offered, should always be delivered in the format popularly known as the "shit sandwich." This triptych of feedback looks like this:

"First, I want to praise what's working here. . . ."
"I think there are opportunities for this work to continue reaching for its highest potential in. . . ."
"But again, my compliments on. . . ."

I can already hear the chorus gathering on social media to shout me down. But aren't we supposed to be *honest*? My teachers demonstrated their brilliance by excoriating me, and I'm a *genius* because of it. Isn't it part of our job to weed out the weaklings?

To them I say this: Feedback that is too broadly, harshly, personally, or forcefully delivered is *not receivable*. If a writer is fighting back tears over a margin note that says, "This is unreadable and unpublishable," he will never be able to hear the voice in the room that says, "The middle section of chapter 2 was giving early Ishiguro; just beautiful work there." If a professor muses to a young writer, "Does the world really need *another* rape memoir?," he silences not just the writer being workshopped that day, but the three other survivors listening carefully to the discussion.

I would also say to the inveterate harshers: Who appointed *you* the little king of everything? Who is any one person to determine what is "publishable"? What is "readable"? Who the "weaklings" are? Speaking only for myself, I have seen writers who I thought had limitless potential go absolutely nowhere professionally, and I have seen writers who I thought were the workshop's weaklings go on to decorated careers. In other words, my first impressions have been mistaken or misleading often enough to instill humility: to convince me that my opinion is only one person's opinion. I've also felt the sting of feedback that was patently unfair, or obviously uninformed, or just glib, lazy, or hurtful. So when I give feedback, I'm always, always starting with a sincere compliment.

As the above rant demonstrates, my MFA experience not only taught me how to give and receive feedback, it also gave me valuable, relational practice in discerning the feedback I could use from the feedback that was of no use to me whatsoever. When I was an undergraduate people-pleaser, I would take home every comment from a workshop and assume it was my duty to incorporate it. It felt like an extreme rebuke to reject a suggestion, and I worried about offending those whose suggestions I ignored. But by the time I reached graduate-level workshops, I realized what suggestions really were: suggestions. Suggestions that I could take or leave as *I* determined would best suit *my* work. I learned that there were trends: Some professors and classmates tended to give more useful feedback, and some were obviously unqualified, for whatever reason, to discuss my work in any depth. And I learned to look for patterns: If three trustworthy interlocutors were highlighting the same problem, then in all likelihood this was a problem to which I should attend.

I learned to take what was useful to me and leave the rest, and now this is most often the language I use to deliver comments to my students: Take whatever's useful from this and leave the rest. The subtext of this, in my mind, is: You will never offend me by making your own creative choices. I want to tell you this explicitly, because there was a time when I didn't know it at all.

Finally, one of the greatest values of my time getting an MFA was that the social immersion of talking to and working with other writers all the time instilled in me a new comfort with the question "What do you do?" The answer felt simpler: "I'm a writer." The MFA doesn't make you a writer, but if you apply yourself wholeheartedly within it, you'll make yourself one.

Now on to my caveats.

The hardest way to receive the MFA question, for me, is when people ask, "Was it worth it?," because my specific program was so obscenely expensive that I think the cost alone made the experience almost unjustifiable.

Cost, in general, is the element of the MFA question that I emphasize most with my students. I usually say something subtle like this: **Do not, do not, do *not*, for any reason, no matter the prestige of the program, go into debt for an MFA.** To do so, in my opinion, is tantamount to paying six figures for a lottery ticket. At Columbia, unsurprisingly, I met many very economically privileged people like me. I also met people who had taken out the maximum loan allotment for tuition *and* the maximum loan allotment for living expenses, because that was the only way they could afford to spend two years studying in New York City. Some of those debts totaled $200,000.

Who can earnestly say that a $200,000 investment in a poetry degree is justified? To be clear, I am *not* here to judge the students in this equation. No, my contempt is reserved for my alma mater. I consider it morally unconscionable that programs such as Columbia's use prestige to compel students to assume debt that their earning potential as novelists or poets or playwrights will simply never recoup. I also think that expensive programs with limited opportunities to defray costs through scholarships or teaching positions fail to foster class and race diversity in their student bodies, and that lack in turn has a devastating impact on the quality of workshop feedback.

For all of these reasons, whenever a student comes into my office hours and asks which MFA programs I think she should apply to, I say, "Only fully funded programs, often but not always at state universities." I make this recommendation regardless of what I suspect this particular student's financial position to be. I contend that funding is a telling indicator of the investment a program is willing to make in a student. It's also a more reliable indicator than, say, whether the author of your favorite book teaches in any given program: Big names tend to spend little time in the classroom, and only a few are as gifted at teaching as they are at writing. I fiercely believe that an MFA should help and not hinder your future earning potential, and that this begins with a debt-free graduation.

Upon finishing my MFA, I also felt sold a bill of goods about my teaching potential. What MFA programs will tell you loud and clear is that you'll need an MFA to teach creative writing at the college or graduate level. This is true, except in select cases where the author holds another advanced degree such as a PhD or even a JD. You may even be able to name a writing professor with nothing more than a bachelor's degree—these exceptions are almost universally members of older generations who have published very celebrated books.

This brings me to the quiet part MFA programs tend to elide in their sales pitch: **You really need an MFA (or another advanced degree) and at least one published book to be taken seriously for institutional teaching positions.** Thus full-time teaching is not usually the first position MFAs obtain upon graduation, even though it is the most emphasized outcome of getting the degree. I hustled for teaching opportunities for *years* before I got that hallowed call from Stanford. Here's a sample of my checkered pedagogical past:

- As an MFA student, I assistant-taught an undergraduate poetry workshop with my wonderful professor Sophie Cabot Black. I made a special request for this opportunity; I believe I was paid a very nominal stipend.
- During my MFA summers, I taught writing in Columbia's summer program for high school students. This paid relatively well.

- On a tip from a friend, I became a teaching assistant for a professor in English and communications at the SEEK program at the John Jay College of Criminal Justice, CUNY. It paid terribly but offered direct, invaluable teaching experience beyond creative writing workshops.

- With *The Beat Within*, the nation's first magazine by and for incarcerated youth, I taught writing in the Santa Clara County juvenile justice facility. I was paid a modest middle-class salary by *The Beat Within*'s parent nonprofit journalism organization, New America Media.

- I taught summer writing classes for teenagers through Upward Bound at Mills College and at the San Francisco School. Maybe a grand or two apiece.

- I coached high schoolers in poetry performance for an organization called California Poetry Out Loud, which facilitates an annual competition something like a spelling bee of poetry recitation. Compensation was nominal, but the opportunity offered me a paid tour of most of San Francisco's public schools, which came in handy once I had kids of my own.

- I taught two evening writing workshops for the San Francisco Writers Grotto, a co-op office space for writers. I received a share of tuition dollars.

- I taught seven rounds of my custom-designed online class "How to Pitch Anything" for Catapult online. I received a notably better share of tuition dollars.

I honestly loved every one of these teaching opportunities, and I'm proud to have taught my craft at so many levels and in so many different environments. But I think it's also important to note that none of these were full-time commitments, none of them paid a sustainable wage, and none of them came with health insurance. This was also true for many of my friends who obtained teaching positions at colleges and universities before I did: Lots of writers string together three or four adjunct jobs at different schools to pay the rent.

All of this is to be candid about what I wish someone had told me when I was plotting my own MFA path: There are simply many more MFA graduates than there are desirable, sustainable university-based jobs teaching creative writing, so the people who get those jobs tend to have distinguished themselves professionally beyond obtaining a graduate degree. You will probably work some crappy, low-paying, entry-level, nondream jobs even with this particular graduate degree in hand. None of these professional realities make you a bad or unsuccessful writer.

So, do I think an MFA can be a valuable vehicle for networking? Of course I do; my professional history clearly evidences that. Do I think that a writer *must* have an MFA to pursue a writing career? I absolutely do not. My MFA program was great for making friends; my writing career was built by putting my ass in a chair and writing.

Get an MFA if you feel called to do so; just don't mortgage your entire future to it. Maintain a clear understanding of what the MFA can do—build your professional network, hone your skills, and deepen your commitment to a life of letters. And maintain an even clearer understanding of what it cannot do—qualify you for a full-time teaching position immediately upon graduation, guarantee you a six-figure book deal, or otherwise plunge you directly into the life of its most famous professor.

ASSIGNMENT

I'd like you to do some light, but active, networking:

- Give two social media shout-outs to other authors—share a great article or book title, tag the author, and write a few words on what you appreciated about it.
- Look at some mastheads and identify three editorial targets at specific publications who you'd like to pitch to in the future.

CHAPTER 4

How to Pitch Short Nonfiction

Personal Essays, Op-Eds, Reported Features, Interviews, Reviews, Roundups, and Cultural Criticism

So. You have polished your author bio; created your website, social media channels, and newsletter; and made yourself findable. You have thoughtfully considered why a particular editor might be likely to be interested in your work, familiarized yourself with their work, and obtained their email address. You have also familiarized yourself with the publication—their submission guidelines, what they do and don't publish, who else writes for them, and, most especially, whether they've recently published a version of your story idea.

All of this means that finally, after all my opining on prepitch preparation, we have arrived at the actual craft of pitching!

But first, lest you assume that this pitching advice is applicable only to people who write nonfiction primarily, and that screenwriters, novelists, and poets can safely ignore it, I caution you. For years, I didn't see myself writing essays either. But it's been my experience that no matter what your primary genre is, having a polished nonfiction voice is an aid to that work. And pitching *is* having a polished nonfiction voice—both require the ability to describe yourself succinctly, effectively, and honestly.

Also, if you're a fiction writer, chances are you'd like to publish a novel or collection of short stories someday, and when you do, your agent and editor will want you to promote that publication with other bylines—a personal story about the inspiration for your book, the long road to selling it, or any other crazy things that happened to you along the way. The same is true with any long-form work—being able to tell engaging true stories about yourself will help audiences get to know you and make them more interested in buying your work. Sure, you'll also do interviews about your project, but you won't get paid for those.

I wish someone had told me that, of all the different genres I've worked in—journalism, poetry, playwriting, fiction, screenwriting—nonfiction would be by far the easiest to monetize. I know so many writers who have found weird, random jobs on Craigslist, then gotten a steady gig writing a column for a newspaper no one's ever heard of, and then landed bigger bylines from there. Relatively speaking, there are more paid opportunities on the internet for first-person essays, reported pieces (news, interviews, cultural criticism, reviews), and nonfiction work that falls somewhere in between than there are for poetry and fiction.

I mention all this because the Literary Industry tends to erect false dichotomies between creative writing and journalism, or between creative and scholarly writing, as if we have to confine ourselves permanently to only one path. But the most successful writers I know can work across those boundaries, and across many others. No one manages to make a living with nothing but a succession of six-figure book deals for novels; many more people make a living in the lulls between big advances by selling short-form work, and much of this paid work is in nonfiction and journalism.

Basic Pitch Template

Excluding your bio, I recommend keeping your pitch between three hundred and five hundred words. Here is a basic structure that you can customize to the publication's guidelines and your voice:

```
Subject: Pitch [or] Submission: "The Pithy, Brief Name
   of My Story"


Hi [first name this person typically uses in their
byline],


Hope this finds you well—I got your email from [mutual
contact, if you have one]. [If you don't have a mutual
contact, just fast-forward to the next paragraph.]
    I'm a great admirer of [any relevant previous work
this editor/publication has done around the general
topic you're pitching: be specific, intelligent, brief,
and complimentary]. In gratitude for/along the same
lines as/to expand on/[another transition that relates
your pitch to the editor's previous work], I'd love to
pitch you a piece [specify its genre: personal essay,
book/film/TV review, interview, cultural criticism,
etc.] that I'm calling "The Pithy, Brief Name of My
```

Story." [*Summarize your story in no more than one to two thesis lines.*]

Here's a brief excerpt to give you a sense of where I'm heading. [*Excerpt one or two polished paragraphs of your piece that get to the core of your idea—what story are you telling, or what argument are you making? If you haven't written the whole essay yet, write two polished paragraphs on the same, introduced with* "I'd like to explore/unpack/examine . . ." *These paragraphs should set out the* **basics** *of your idea or a relevant anecdote that evokes it (what is obvious to you and what the reader may already know about the subject), then* **dive further** *into the subject (what else you know and what may surprise the reader about the subject), and land with* **some interesting questions** *that leave the editor wanting to read more—why should they care?* "Tease the third act," *as a fellowship reader once told me.*]

[*Conclude with a brief paragraph that* **links to any other recent, relevant writing** *you've done on this subject,* **provides a rough ballpark of the word count you're imagining** *for your piece (which should take into account the typical length of other pieces in this publication), and* **thanks** *the editor again for their time and consideration.*]

Sincerely / all best / your preferred sign-off,

[*Your name*]

[*Your medium-length author bio*]

How to Write Your Cold Pitch

Most of the terminology I use in this section assumes that you are pitching a piece of short nonfiction to an editor you don't know at an online publication, but the information is also applicable to pitching in any genre or professional context.

There are three massively important principles of pitching a creative idea to a busy stranger.

- Have an **ask.** Be specific about why you're writing and what you want.
- Be **brief** and **compelling.** Get right to the point, make the point intriguing, and then get out.
- **Do not apologize.**

Address the editor by whatever they commonly go by on the internet. First names are usually fine, but it's also fine to use an honorific. I'll note here that the first-name "Hi Laura" convention in media and publishing differs somewhat from the more formal "Dear Professor Goode" conventions of academia.

"Should I write the pitch or the story first?" is the great chicken-or-egg question of pitching! Rather than trying to provide a one-size-fits-all prescription here, I'll note that in my own experience the answer has fluctuated on a story-by-story basis.

The main argument for writing the pitch first is that this route can avoid unpaid work, which sometimes includes reporting and research as well as writing. The guiding principle of pitching is that you're throwing out an interesting but unfinished idea. A great pitch offers an idea with enough structure and heft to make it convincing, and enough open-endedness to allow the editor a say in the idea's execution. It's been my experience that editors tend to prefer this opportunity for involvement, and that involving a good editor early in the process usually results in a tighter story.

However, many writers panic at this counsel, because how are we supposed to crystallize a polished pitch before we even know what story we're writing? Take three deep breaths: It is perfectly fine to write a full-story draft before distilling its pitch. This will take more of your time, yes, but that time can be well spent if it helps you generate a stronger, more informed pitch.

Just as every story process is different—influenced by the mood, information, available time, and eccentricities of the moment—every pitch process is different. Let it be.

So how do we turn an inchoate idea into a tight pitch and, eventually, into a compelling story? I like to think of the process of generating a story idea as a process of addressing this question: What is obvious to me that may not be obvious to everyone? At the topical level, consider the question "What's my beat?" What is/ are the general area(s) of subject matter that interests me most? What obsesses me? Recall Alexander Chee's question: Dying, what stories would you tell? What you think of as your beat should be what absorbs you in your free time. These deep, genuine, abiding interests will allow you to draw quickly and authoritatively on an organic store of knowledge.

Within your broader area of interest, start taking some notes on a specific idea, and don't stop until you have two paragraphs of *something*. Sometimes what results will be the essay itself, sometimes it'll become a more crystallized central concept to propose in a pitch, sometimes it'll lead nowhere but will have taken you down an interesting rabbit hole for a few hours. That's writing.

Sometimes I manipulate myself into getting started: I have an internal conversation that goes something like "Okay, Laura, I know you're a no-talent garbage fire, but what if you impersonated a capable writer for, say, half an hour? What if you just pretended, for the purposes of these thirty minutes, that you were equal to this task?" More often than not, writing flows from this predicate.

Your job in writing an effective pitch is to answer three questions:

- What does an audience likely already know about this subject?
- What about this subject may surprise them?
- Why should they care?

Say that you've reasoned through the chicken-or-egg conundrum and determined that you definitely cannot come up with a pitch without writing a full draft of the story first. You may next feel tempted just to send out that story draft, rather than distilling it into a pitch. However, I would advise against sending a full story in an initial outreach to an editor you don't know, otherwise known as a *cold pitch*. (If you've worked previously with the editor, then opening with a full draft is safer.) Even if you have a full draft on hand, use your pitch to tantalize the editor with just a few paragraphs that excerpt and encapsulate the story, and offer to send more if they're interested.

I make this recommendation on the basis of the following calculation: If your excerpted paragraphs are smart and expandable, then you look intriguing. If you send a full essay right off the bat that has a promising thesis but ultimately reads to the editor as too long or colloquial or specious, you risk losing the editor's interest because they can't picture it in their publication. Holding back the full essay is the editorial equivalent of leaving something to the imagination.

If you're pitching a story on a subject that you've never written about before, don't assume that you're underqualified and must bend over backward to prove yourself. A pitch is where you demonstrate your capacity to expand on an interesting idea or argument. If your pitch takes an editor through your thesis statement and core question, and all the ways you plan to develop it, then you don't need to have written one hundred articles on the subject already, because you'll have just made a convincing case for how you'll shape this story effectively.

Write the pitch in a tone that feels authentic to you and representative of the piece you'd like to write. In other words, be yourself, but demonstrate that you're familiar with this gatekeeper's body of work. Also, hearkening back to avoiding apology, and everything else we've been talking about with regard to the performance of confidence, do your best to present a confident tone.

If you want to drop a name of a mutual connection in your pitch, check in with the mutual friend first to get their consent—or better yet, ask them to tee up an e-intro for you. After obtaining that consent, I usually name-drop in the opening of a pitch email: for example, "So-and-so suggested I might get in touch with you about . . ." or "I loved the work you did with my friend so-and-so on . . ."

It can be savvy, for your first pitch to a new editorial contact, to keep the proposed story on the shorter side. This often makes it easier for the editor to say yes. Especially for those of you who don't have a ton of clips online, pitching short, tight pieces is appealing to editors because it's less risky for them in terms of budget and page space. These days, most places love to get pieces that are 800 to 1,200 words, and it can be harder to find places that are willing to go north of 1,500 unless you have a very compelling story. I'd call "short" the 800- to 1,000-word range. Features of

5,000 words are the most desirable jobs and tend to go to the most recognizable, established people. It's good practice to get a solid grasp on the craft of a 1,000- to 1,500-word piece before you attempt to get your arms around a 3,000- to 4,000-word one; similarly, an editor who's been impressed with how well you executed on a 1,000-word piece may entrust you with a 2,000-word one in the future.

Speaking of word counts, **it is important to specify an estimated word count in your pitch, usually toward the pitch's conclusion.** At least specify a range: 700–800 words, 1,500–1,800 words, and so on.

You will also modulate the length of the pitch somewhat, depending on the publication and topic. You buy yourself some license for length if there's background you need to set up—say, for something heavily researched or reported—or complexity you're trying to address. But most of the time, editors are going to be most responsive to something quick and pithy. In other words, if your pitch runs extra-long, it had better be extra-good.

You want to reveal the answers to a few of your story's big questions in your pitch, but not all of them. Dangle. Tantalize. Set up acts 1 and 2 of your story and just tease act 3. Give a little background, connect to a news hook, introduce your argument, drop a shocking fact or two, and build up to some interesting but unanswered questions.

If you're pitching an interview, a profile, or anything else that requires both an editor's and a subject's consensual participation, then who to contact first can become another chicken-or-egg question. I recommend starting with whichever contact you know better.

These kinds of stories will, in all likelihood, involve some people you know personally. Some top-tier publications—traditional newspapers such as *The New York Times*—will "full disclosure" any personal relationship between writer and subject, but most of the time, this is a shamelessly nepotistic and incestuous industry. Presenting yourself as well connected is generally something editors like.

If your pitch is pegged to an upcoming cultural event (a season premiere, an opening night, a publication date), then pitch the editor four to eight weeks ahead of time, give or take. You'll need enough time to do an interview or review the material, but probably not more than three months ahead of the relevant date.

In traditional publishing, I've noticed that editors tend to be less responsive in August, in December/January (around the holidays), and in the summer generally. I recommend sending pitches during business hours, when they're likeliest to be seen. If you send something on Saturday night, then it may get buried in the eighty-nine other emails that the editor opens first thing Monday morning. Your email program's "schedule send" feature is a godsend for timing your pitches.

TAILORING YOUR PITCH TO ITS TARGET

I am far from the world's sole authority on all of this: There is a wealth of tips and tricks on pitching on the internet. There are so many tips out there, in fact, that before you pitch any editor at any publication, I recommend doing an online search for "[Publication] tips for pitching."

Finally: What, exactly, do I mean by "Do not apologize"? Actors are trained never to apologize for an audition, and the same principle applies to writers while pitching. When you are granted five minutes to impress a busy gatekeeper into giving you an opportunity, do *not* spend three of them explaining that you've got a bit of a cold, and traffic was awful on the way here, and you may not be in your greatest voice today. Instead, no matter how you got there, your job is to get your hair out of your face, smile wide, and belt like God is listening. When someone asks you for a song, you do not say, "I'm sorry." You say, "Broadway, Disney, church, or radio?" If your voice cracks, you keep singing. If you fall on your ass, you make it funny. There is a notorious Hollywood story about how Lea Michele got into a car accident on the way to her *Glee* audition, arrived literally picking glass shards out of her hair, and still nailed it. So when I say, "Do not apologize," I mean: Write pitches that take no prisoners, can be deterred by no earthly force, and are only made more dazzling by their lingering glass shards.

Successful Pitch Examples

Here are two of my pitches that were accepted and became stories at *Glamour* and *BuzzFeed Reader,* respectively. In the first pitch to *Glamour,* for a personal essay, I'd worked with the editor before at a different publication, so my tone is colloquial, and I don't include introductory info such as my bio or website. The second, for an extensively reported piece of cultural criticism, was a cold pitch to an editor at *BuzzFeed* to whom I was vaguely connected in the feminist-writer internetosphere, but whom I didn't know personally. Because I didn't know the editor and was proposing a research-heavy piece, the *BuzzFeed* pitch is longer and does include that introductory info.

Personal Essay Pitch for *Glamour*

Subject: Pitch: I quit breastfeeding because it sucked

Hey [editor],

I just quit breastfeeding at eight weeks with my shiny new second baby because breastfeeding sucked for me. Even though breastfeeding "worked" this time, it was still a matter of bloody nipples, spending forty-five to sixty of my (his) every waking ninety minutes trapped under a baby, having almost no time or attention to give to my older child, and giving up every shred of my freedom. By the time we had introduced enough formula to observe how much better the baby was sleeping on it, nursing's days were clearly numbered. I'm gaga in love with my baby, but I *hated* breastfeeding.

I'm still battling some guilt about all this, but it hits me as a potential story idea for you: I haven't read many/almost any personal essays about actively *choosing* not to breastfeed, as opposed to just not being *able* to breastfeed, like I wrote about my experience with my first child in my formula story for *R29* last year. I feel like so many women confess in these hushed tones about how hard breastfeeding can be but then still guilt themselves into suffering through it, and there needs to be more of a public dialogue supporting a range of feeding choices. For instance,

I'm obsessed with Nicole Cliffe's tweets on the subject (with a little cameo from yours truly in that Storify link).

Could you give me like 1,200 to 1,500 words for something like this? The lactivists would certainly come for me on it, but that can't be terrible for page views! I won't stop until La Leche League creates a blacklist just for me.

Hope you're really well! Would love to work with you on this or something else soon.

Thanks so much,

L.

Heavily Reported Cultural Criticism Pitch for
BuzzFeed Reader

Subject: Feature pitch: The radical evolution of
Lifetime: Television for Women

Hey [editor],

I hope this finds you well! I'm a longtime reader of
[your past publication] and am excited to see your
transition to *BuzzFeed*! Like you, I toggle between the
film and literary worlds, and as such, hoped you might
be interested in an investigative/critical feature I've
been wanting to write.

I'd like to explore what I see as the radical
evolution of Lifetime: Television for Women in a way
that takes the network, its history, its audience, and
its current content seriously as part of our feminist
cultural conversation. With Lifetime's summer 2015
breakout hit *UnREAL,* as well as its increasingly avant-
garde forays into self-parodying its own film genre, the
network has recently followed two decades of
establishing a distinctive brand of shlocky women's
entertainment with what seems to be a postmodern
commentary on that brand as an evolving feminist genre.
What's more, Lifetime recently pledged to hire any
female AFI grad who wants a job with the network: an
action that both recognizes Lifetime's unique position

to address the abysmal hiring numbers for female filmmakers and pointedly notes that Lifetime has been hiring more women than other networks all along.

UnREAL is no doubt both the centerpiece and the catalyst of much of this transformation, and the fact that Constance Zimmer just won a Critic's Choice Award for her work on the series marks a real sea change for both UnREAL and Lifetime's critical estimation. UnREAL is both messy and trashy in a manner that reinforces Lifetime's original brand conception, and is also prestigious in a way that expands, challenges, and reinvents that brand image. UnREAL co-creator Sarah Gertrude Shapiro is no small part of this delightful mess; in her wildly entertaining TED Talk "How to Borrow Male Privilege in Hollywood," for one, she describes getting drunk and hiring a friend to pose as her male assistant in order to get her first meeting with a big Hollywood lawyer. (I love this woman.) Lifetime took a big risk on Shapiro; she sold UnREAL to the network on a single pitch with no agent, but it seems to be paying dividends.

All of this prompts the question: Was Lifetime always as terrible as we thought it was—even the most brilliant cultural critic in the world, Roxane Gay, cops willingly to her love for Lifetime movies—or is our own internalized misogyny to blame for dismissing its content as soap, as froth, as shlock? Can the network reinvent itself without alienating its advertisers or core audience? If Lifetime delivers on its promise to take risks on promising female film school grads, could it even build upon its brand in order to claim new ground for feminism on television? I'd like to investigate: by interviewing Shapiro and her *UnREAL* co-creator Marti Noxon, by interviewing some Lifetime executives, by reviewing some of its high-profile 2015 programming, and hopefully by getting some exclusive scoop on what they have in the pipeline.

I wrote about *UnREAL* for *Bright Ideas* magazine when the show first premiered, and more recently did a short follow-up interview with Shapiro for *Bright Ideas'*s next print issue (premiering at Sundance), so I have a good relationship with Lifetime's publicity director, and with some lead time I think I could work with her to get access to a wider swath of their key players. I'd love to lean into a piece like this with some length—like 2,000-4,000 words.

Thanks so much for your consideration—I'd be delighted to hear any feedback you might have on this idea, as I would be to find any excuse whatsoever to work with you. I'm including my standard author bio below for your reference, and sending you every good wish!

All best to you,

L.

[Medium-length author bio]

What Happens After You Send Your Pitch

There is a maddening and near-total lack of standardized response times on pitches; these vary widely by venue. I've had editors get back to me in twenty-four hours and I've had them get back to me in six months. It totally depends. In most cases, though, editors will move quickly on something that interests them.

Unless a piece is very timely, in which case I think it's valid to follow up within a few days, I'd send a follow-up after two to four weeks, or whenever the publication specifies. Read the publication's submission guidelines and see if they list a "if you don't hear from us by X weeks, assume we've passed," or a "feel free to follow up after X weeks," but absent those specific guidelines, two to four weeks is fine. If I haven't heard from a publication after a month, and they don't say anything specific in their guidelines, I usually assume it's a pass.

There exists some light controversy in magazine publishing about **simultaneous submissions.** Which is to say: Is it good or bad form to pitch to more than one editor simultaneously?

First, the official rules: Many places will note in their submission guidelines whether they accept simultaneous submissions or not. If the publication doesn't specify, then they accept simultaneous submissions by default.

Now the unofficial rules: I think simultaneous pitching makes sense when the story is very timely and the author still takes care to customize each pitch to its target. In this scenario, it may sometimes, though not always, make sense to be explicit in the pitch itself that you're going out to multiple editors with this story.

What I absolutely, 100 percent do not recommend is mass-blasting the exact same nonfiction pitch to twenty editors at a time. Editors can tell when a pitch is generic, and targeting will get you much farther than mass-blasting, even if math seems to indicate otherwise.

Now I will directly contradict myself: For poetry and short fiction, mass-blast all you want. Some literary magazines get prickly about simultaneous submissions, but my contention is that they don't pay enough, and can't respond quickly enough, to demand proprietary hold over all *potential* publications. It's still wise to notify publications if your piece gets accepted elsewhere, and notifying a non-sim-sub publication that you've sim-subbed and gotten published elsewhere could, I suppose, alienate them. But they didn't publish you anyway, right?

For more evergreen stories (i.e., most personal essays), I like to give editor #1 a few weeks to respond before moving on to editor #2. Then, particularly if I have a relationship with editor #1, I might send them a quick check-in like "Hey, I just wanted to follow up, are you still considering this? As a heads-up, if I don't hear from you by EOD tomorrow, I'm going to pitch elsewhere." If I don't have a relationship with editor #1, I'll just move on to pitching someone else and circle back to check in with editor #1 only if editor #2 makes an offer. In that desirable event, my email would be more like "Hey, I've had some interest in this piece, but I was still curious to hear your thoughts on it—could you let me know in the next twenty-four hours if you're still considering it?"

Please do yourself a favor and **keep track of your pitches.** Online trackers such as Submittable and Duotrope both serve this purpose. I maintain a running spreadsheet where I record every submission I send, including story title, editor (and editor's email address), publication, date, whether the publication accepts simultaneous submissions, and submission status; and for accepted stories, the payment due, date I invoiced for payment, and date payment is received. It looks like this:

Essay/Pitch	Publication	Editor	Date	Sim Subs?	Results	Payment Due	Invoiced	Payment Rec'd?
My Teen Mom Feeling	ELLE	Chloe Schama	12/29/2015	No	YES	$300	1/12/2016	3/14/2016
Interview with James Kaelan	Bright Ideas	Nicole Malek	1/1/2016	No	YES	$200	1/15/2016	3/28/2016

This record is helpful for all manner of things: keeping track of editorial contacts, rounding up tax information, keeping your bio and website current, and, most important, making sure you get paid what you're owed on time. I'll revisit all this in more detail when I cover negotiating, getting paid, and staying organized in chapter 8.

Your Pitch Was Accepted, Yay!

Just like editorial response times, editorial pay scales are far-ranging and nonstandardized. **To determine how much money to ask for, consult** whopayswriters.com, **consider what you've been paid for similar pieces in the past (if possible), and ask friends who've written for said publication how much they've been paid.** Consider word count, depth of reporting/research, and timeliness.

Make sure payment is discussed after the pitch and before the byline: Usually I bring up money in my response to an editor's acceptance unless they mention it directly in the acceptance. An initial pitch rarely includes a price tag, but the price tag should be discussed soon after the pitch is accepted. Make sure payment is discussed before the piece gets close to pubbing, before you move from pitch to draft, and before anyone tries to get you to sign a contract. *Do not* assume that the editor will bring it up or that there is no money available if they haven't mentioned it. Again, rest assured that we will revisit my passion for informed negotiation in just a few chapters.

As you compose your pitch and envision your story, you should also **develop a realistic timeline for how long it will take you to complete the story** and include this in your editorial communications. *Don't* assume that as soon as your editor accepts a pitch, it automatically becomes a race to finish the piece. Unless a story is very timely, in which case you should ask for rush-rate money to finish it quickly, editors will usually just ask you how much time you need to write the story. If it doesn't require heavy reporting, a week or two is probably fine. If it requires more reporting, give your best estimate of how much time you'll need, and stay in touch as you progress. In general, just be realistic and communicative about the time you need.

Sometimes an editor will respond to the effect of "I'm intrigued, but I'd like you to consider A and B, reconsider C, and have you thought about adding a light splash of D?" What they really mean is "I think your story idea is compelling enough to invest some time in this conversation, but I need you to audition a little more before I'm going to make you an offer." This is a promising type of response, and just invites you to keep pitching.

There's also more lenience regarding the length of your pitch if you get this kind of response—if an editor invites your further thoughts, feel free to expand . . . more expansively. But depending on how quickly the editor got back to you, the amount of work they're asking for, and how newsy the story is, this is a situation where a quicker response to them holds virtue—twenty-four hours or less, barring extenuating circumstances. If an editor is writing you back, they're already considering moving forward with the story, so make it easy for them to turn their maybe into a yes.

This also supports the argument for front-loading the time you need to make the original pitch really tight—if all goes well, the process will typically move faster from there, so you want to be operating from a strong foundation.

Most editors will at least welcome suggestions for **headlines for your story,** so it's a fantastic idea to file your first draft with a few suggestions for potential headlines (the main text at the top of the page) and deks (the italicized, slightly longer subheader). This shows editors that you know what your main idea is and how the publishing process goes, and most endearingly of all, it also may save them work. Writing headlines and deks can help you to crystallize the core of your story for yourself.

All of that said, in many cases, your stories will run under headlines you didn't write, and sometimes under headlines you *never* would have written. Editors at online publications, particularly, will often generate their own most clickable headlines. Some publications literally have a digital headline generator. A few very established authors—Rachel Kaadzi Ghansah has my permanent respect for this—have a personal policy about writing their own headlines, but this kind of clout takes Ghansah-level talent and experience to earn.

Overall, speaking from my own personal experience, I've seen some of my stories run with terrible headlines even in otherwise great and rewarding editorial relationships. The best we can do is offer up our best ideas proactively and not take it personally when the clickbait wins.

It also does sometimes happen that a pitch is accepted and

then the draft is rejected. It's unusual for stories to be killed after pitches are accepted, but far from unheard of. In my experience, happily, this has happened less because the draft I filed was god-awful and more because of external factors—a key source falls through, a similar story appears, a publication changes owner-ship.

If the publication is established enough (i.e., owned by any sort of corporation), then the contract you sign for your piece may stipulate a **kill fee,** also known as the amount you'll be paid for your work if the accepted piece doesn't go to publication. Often the kill fee is 25 percent of the agreed-upon price of the piece. The kill fee is a good thing to look for, or negotiate for, when reading contracts (again, more on this in chapter 8).

If a story gets killed, as with all things, do your best not to take it personally, and remain as cordial and professional as possible with your editorial contact.

Here's a sort-of-funny anecdote about a story of mine that got killed. In fall 2016, a friend of a friend reached out and asked me to write a feature for a techie publication that was on my radar but not in my usual editorial orbit. The story she proposed was about cross-political reconciliation and healing leading up to the 2016 presidential election. (Yeah, I know, I can hear you laughing.) I dutifully tried to find sources for such a narrative but discovered instead that everyone with politically mixed families was *really* pissed at their relatives. Then the 2016 presidential election hap-pened and made the reconciliation-and-healing angle catastroph-ically infeasible. We tried to re-angle the story a few times, but at the same time the publication gained a new editor in chief with a totally new editorial mandate. Though neither my editor nor I did anything wrong, my story died a slow, many-drafted death. I still managed to get paid for it, and I still have tremendous respect for the editor who commissioned me. No harm, no foul, shit happens. And fuck Donald Trump.

ASSIGNMENT

- Build your **submissions tracker** in Excel, Sheets, or your preferred program, or use an online tracker such as Submittable or Duotrope.
- Write a **draft pitch**—two to five paragraphs plus a short/ medium bio—of a short nonfiction piece, aimed at one of the target editors you identified in your last assignment. You can pitch a **personal essay, news story, review, cultural critique, or interview.** Introduce yourself and your work with confidence!

CHAPTER 5

Querying Agents for Long-Form Work

Novels, Memoirs, Short Stories, and Essay Collections

All of the same assets—your author bio, website, newsletter, and generally findable internet presence—that you built to pitch short-form pieces to editors will be valuable when you want to sell a book, which usually requires finding an **agent** first to market your book to editors/publishers. In this chapter, I focus on that process: querying a literary agent for a book.*

In addition to finding new authors through referrals, viral stories, and personal solicitations, literary agents find new authors through what's called the "query" process. At the heart of this process is the **query letter,** and at the heart of the query letter itself is your **story synopsis.**

---

*   A minor disclaimer: The publishing apparatus of illustrated children's books tends to operate somewhat distinctly from that of adult books. The tips for querying agents in this chapter will still apply to the process of seeking representation for a children's, middle grade, or young adult novel. However, I recommend that authors seeking representation for illustrated or picture books for early readers consult another resource.

A reminder: **Agents pitch books to editors/publishers. Authors do not pitch books directly to editors/publishers.** There are a few exceptions to this procedure—very small presses, contests, personal relationships—but in the vast majority of cases, it's a waste of your time to send your manuscript directly to editors/publishers. You'll end up in the slush pile (see page 40), where occasionally a manuscript will shoot the moon and get published, but where 99 percent of manuscripts go to die a whimpering death. Spend your time finding your manuscript an agent, or even plotting a tight self-publishing plan, instead.

Preparing to Find an Agent

While you're determining which agents to query, many of the same principles of short-form pitching will apply: Do your research on each individual's online presence, read submissions guidelines, root out e-introductions where you can, and be prepared to make an argument for why your work is a good fit for your target's interests.

The single best source of actionable agent information, I've found, is the **acknowledgments pages** of your favorite authors' books. Authors always, whether out of real gratitude or decorum, thank their agents and editors here, and they also often thank editors and publications who first published individual essays or stories in a collection, writer friends who read an early draft, or mentors who were especially generous. Read acknowledgments and credits carefully: It is valuable to you to know who is associated with whom, and if you're anything like me, it's also fun to imagine who's friends with whom.

For some more insider information, I recommend agent Kate McKean's newsletter *Agents and Books*, and the *Publishers Mar-*

ketplace Writer's Guide, which I discovered in Kate's newsletter, and which describes in detail how you can use Publishers Marketplace (a publishing industry news website) to collect agent information.

Because writers are never really done with our work, it can be hard to figure out how Finished is Finished Enough to start sharing our manuscript with agents. At the high level, you have much more to lose by querying too early than you do by querying later, so I encourage first-time authors, in particular, to take your time. I say this knowing I'll repeat it: **Agents will only read your work once.** So take the time to show them your most polished work. One misplaced comma probably isn't going to make or break an agent's decision about your manuscript, but these professionals are extremely keen at identifying the difference between an author who's put in the necessary work and an amateur who hasn't—it's important to proof adequately for grammar, structure, continuity, and the like.

If you are a **fiction** writer preparing to query agents for a first novel or short story collection, my rule of thumb is that the manuscript should be finished, or **no less than three drafts** into completion. I define *draft* as a pass through the manuscript after which you have fixed everything that you can see needs fixing. After this, you show the manuscript to a trusted reader, who will point out ten thousand other things that you missed on your own pass. Then you do it again.

I define *finished* by the metric Melissa Febos offers in her excellent craft book *Body Work:*

> You know when something is done, I tell them (they always want to know how to know when something is done), when you know the argument for every single choice,

when not a single apostrophe has slipped by uninterrogated, when every word has been swapped for its synonym and then recovered.

It's also worth acknowledging that agents and editors are understandably warier of taking on an unproven author—talent is eye-catching, but even more compelling is empirical evidence that this author has the capacity to finish writing a book, preferably even a good book, and debut authors simply have not yet demonstrated this capacity. All of this is to say: If you're a first-time author querying agents for a novel, finish the book before you start querying.

If you are a **nonfiction** writer (or a non-debut fiction writer with a strong sales record), it's likelier that you'll be able to sell your book on a proposal. This proposal should be every bit as polished as the recommendation I offered fiction writers: Don't skimp on collecting feedback and drafting meticulously.

A book proposal, generally speaking, is a sample of several chapters from the book, along with assets that demonstrate where the book is headed: An overview of the book as a whole, a table of contents, brief outlines of each unwritten chapter, works that could be compared to your book (comps), and an estimate of the time you think you'll need to finish writing it. A compelling book proposal will also include some marketing information: your author bio, website, social media statistics, previous publications, and praise from others. (We will revisit the subject of book proposals in much more depth in the next chapter.)

Platform tends to matter more with nonfiction than with fiction. A nonfiction book proposal should demonstrate a strong online presence, verified expertise in your subject area—like speaking gigs and previous publications—and a strategy for reaching your core audience. (Remember when I recommended that you start a newsletter long before ever publishing a book?) If your platform is less developed, it may be a good use of your time to finish the whole book before querying agents.

Ask for help with this. Unless a manuscript has already been workshopped heavily in a graduate program or another kind of class, then you absolutely need *someone* beyond you to have laid eyes on it before you blast it to the professionals. I'd recommend recruiting at least two competent readers, on different drafts, to give you a round of notes that's as comprehensive as possible.

My best advice on finding your best readers:

- Be a fantastic, reliable reader yourself. When a friend asks you for notes, come through on time and in detail. Honing your editing instincts will sharpen your own work too.
- Barter rounds of notes: It's easiest to ask a favor if you're offering one in return. "Hey friend, how's your novel going? I'd be glad to give you a round of notes if that would be helpful, because I'm trying to query agents in about three months, and I need some notes *bad*."
- I will never stop yammering about community: Putting significant time into building yours will generate great readers. Classes, degree or nondegree, are often a fantastic portal to mutually beneficial literary friendships—so, too, are conferences, writing groups, and online communities such as NaNoWriMo (National Novel Writing Month).
- Notice how people respond to your requests for notes. If a friend ghosts you on your request or gives unhelpful feedback, then don't ask that friend to read again. If a

friend takes your work seriously and gives you fantastic notes, then go out of your way to reciprocate.

- If you don't have someone in your life who'll give you a round of notes for free, hire a professional editor; a few hundred dollars in this department usually amounts to money very well spent. Many, many authors advertise editing services on their websites, and it's easy to ask for recommendations on social media too.

- Once you've done this hard work of asking for feedback and incorporating it, you're in a good position to send your first round of agent queries. **I strongly recommend assembling an initial query round of no more than three to five agents, culled from personal connections and acknowledgment pages of authors you love.** If that first round of queries doesn't yield a connection—that's very common; don't be discouraged!—then proceed with querying in further rounds of three to five agents at a time. Some agents will indicate on their websites that a nonresponse beyond X weeks is equivalent to a pass. I would allocate up to twelve weeks to each submission round; don't send a new round until you've heard from all previous editors or passed their pass-by-silence stop date.

Why do I feel so strongly about three to five agents at a time? It's easy to assume that the more agents you pitch, the likelier you are to get a yes—but as with other pitching, a targeted approach will usually get you farther than just casting the widest possible net. You may receive excellent feedback on your unpublished manuscript from agents, and later editors, who pass on it. Or you may have a revelation about your story at some point in the querying process that leads to a breakthrough revision. If you want to keep putting your best work out into the world, that work will necessarily change over time.

Remember: **Agents will only read your query, or any part of your book, once.** To outline the worst-case scenario: You don't want to mass-blast the first draft of your query and chapter(s) to your twenty dream agents, get a piece of revelation-inducing feedback from one of them—or catch a glaring typo on page 2, or a plot hole on page 40—and then realize that you could have showed nineteen other agents better work if you'd been more patient with the process. It may take longer, but it's strategic to query in four batches of three to five agents at a time, incorporating the feedback from each submission round along the way. Also, you'll get better at pitching the more you pitch, so it can be strategic to start with less experienced agents for practice first and save your dream agents for later.

As you assemble your query package, you'll want to look up the websites and submission pages of any prospective agent targets for instructions: Are they currently open for submissions, what genres do they represent, do they list any topics of special interest, and do they specify a preferred submission procedure? Make sure you **follow each agent's query guidelines carefully,** paying especially close attention to making sure that they represent your intended genre, whether it's okay to query another agent at their agency simultaneously, what length and format they request, and what their typical response time and procedure are.

For example, here's an excerpt from my friend John Cusick's query page:

JOHN CUSICK

FOLIO LITERARY MANAGEMENT

WHAT I'M LOOKING FOR: I'm seeking unique voices in middle-grade, young adult, and YA/adult-crossover fiction, as well as adult sci-fi, fantasy, and horror. I want stories that move readers, moments that make me look up and say "Wow, yes. I've felt that."

I want compelling page-turners that create lifelong readers, stories that will inspire fandoms, characters readers will cosplay as, obsess over, and never forget. I want #ownvoices stories of all styles and genres, and am particularly interested in sci-fi, fantasy, and genre fiction from underrepresented voices. I love the strange, iconoclastic, and unusual. Send me the books kids will sneak/steal/borrow in secret. Those intimate, dangerous, lifesaving stories.

I love proactive protagonists, kids and teens chasing a dream or a hero who swings in with a song in her heart and a knife in her teeth.

WHAT I'M NOT LOOKING FOR: I am not seeking picture book authors or illustrators, or nonfiction, at this time.

HOW I WORK: As a writer myself, I bring both a creative and commercial sensibility to my agenting style. I'm an editorial agent who works closely with my clients, whether it's developing a debut project or helping a seasoned author take their next step. My goal is to match writers with their dream editor, secure the best deals possible, facilitate the exploitation of dramatic (film and TV) rights in my clients' work, and grow authors' readership over long careers.

Different agents will specify different preferences (2,500 words, one to three chapters, chapters attached versus pasted in body of email, etc.) that you should follow to the letter: Part of the assignment here is demonstrating that you understand the assignment. In the absence of stated specific preferences, **the industry standard for an agent query is a one-page letter and the first chapter (around twenty pages) of your book, all pasted in the body of an email.** If the agent is interested in reading your whole manuscript, they'll respond to request it.

Just as you made a submission tracker for your short pitches (see page 74), it is a fantastic idea to make a submissions tracker for your agent queries, including the agent's name, the agency they work for, the date you submitted, and a note about their submission guidelines. I would start building this document while you're collecting agent information from acknowledgments pages and personal contacts. Update it regularly: When you get a pass, cross a pass-by-silence date, or get interested in a new agent.

Writing Your Query Letter

Your query package for agents will consist of two essential elements: your manuscript/proposal and a query letter. The basic structure of your query letter will closely follow the basic pitching structure we discussed in chapter 4—you want to introduce yourself with confidence, grab your reader's attention with your quality of thought, relate your work to their previous work, and include a brief summary of your career highlights. There is a wealth of successful query examples on the internet! Writer's Digest, for example, has published more than sixty successful query letters, commented on by the agents who accepted them.

Your query letter radiates around its core element: a tight,

propulsive summary of your book, packed into no more than one or two paragraphs. Past the core synopsis paragraphs, there are some other technical things your query letter should cover. Clearly note the **genre, length** (in words or page count), and **stage of completion** of the project. Specify what **audience** your work targets. Are you writing a young adult novel, and if so, is it aimed at elementary schoolers, preteens (usually called middle-grade in industry language), or teenagers? Does your memoir address an issue that affects twenty-five million Americans? Will fans of X bestselling author connect with your work? Who did you write this work for? Your letter should also make a strong argument for **how your project is a great fit for its recipient.** This is usually achieved by detailing how your novel is realistically comparable to the other books and authors this agent represents.

To put this general language into a more specific frame, below is a template query letter. For fun, I get to play the agent here.

Dear Ms. Goode,

You seem like someone who would be interested in an unreliable narrator's twisty tale of assumed identity, class mobility, and lost love dashed upon the rocks of the Long Island Sound. Like you, I grew up in the Twin Cities, then attended college on the East Coast. I'd be most grateful if you'd consider representing my novel *The Great Gatsby* (working title).

The Great Gatsby is a 47,000-word Jazz Age literary novel narrated by a secondary character, gimlet-eyed Nick Carraway. When Nick moves to glittering West Egg, he meets neighbor Jay Gatsby, who seems still to be awfully torn up over an old flame from his Southern youth, onetime debutante Daisy Buchanan. Daisy is now married to the buffoon Tom Buchanan, but Nick and Jay's conspicuously close duo manages to reunite Jay and Daisy. Tragedy strikes when Tom discovers the affair and confronts Jay, revealing a crucial secret: While Jay portrays himself as an effete, educated, and legitimate businessman, he's actually a rags-to-riches poser who made his fortune bootlegging. Will Daisy choose Jay's newfangled, if invented, version of American prosperity, or stand by her old-money husband even though he's mean and racist? If Dostoevsky said that every story in literature reduces ultimately to "a man goes on a journey" or "a stranger comes to town," *Gatsby* aspires to both, adding dramatic car crashes to connect them. Who will survive the wreckage?

The Great Gatsby will captivate readers of my previous two novels, *This Side of Paradise* and *The Beautiful and The Damned,* as well as those of John Dos Passos's *Manhattan Transfer.* I received my BA from Princeton University, where I found myself subtly unadaptable to Eastern life, and I am a veteran of the U.S. Army. My short fiction has previously appeared in the *Princeton Tiger,* the *Nassau Lit,* and more recently *The Saturday Evening Post.* This is a simultaneous submission, and I'm including the first 2,500 words of *Gatsby.* Thank you most sincerely for your consideration.

Gratefully yours,

Scott Fitzgerald

Note that this query:

- Is brief and to the point, around one page.
- Includes comparable titles, or "comps"—books that are in some way reminiscent of the writer's. These can include inspirations, influences, or best of all, other books or authors represented by this agent.
- Clearly indicates the length and genre of the manuscript.
- Gives specific reasoning for why they think this agent would be interested in their work.
- Focuses on the plot of the novel's story, rather than offering long, heady descriptions of its themes.
- Highlights a few relevant, impressive biographical details without writing an extensive life story. I also think it's okay for a query writer to include the medium version of their bio at the foot of the letter.
- Clearly indicates that this manuscript is under consideration elsewhere ("simultaneous submission").
- Describes the novel in just one paragraph that teases interest in the whole book.

WHAT ARE COMPS AND HOW DO I SELECT THEM?

Comp is an industry term that means "comparable or competitive work," and it's a power tool for building a clear, vivid picture of your manuscript. Metaphor is empathy's ally, so describing your book in relation to three other works your reader loved can build a connection between them and your book.

Do some research on comps, but don't try too hard to connect your book to works that are prestigious. An ideal comp is a book published within the last five years that has already spoken to you deeply. Comps are also a handy tool for demonstrating a book's marketability: They are books you highlight as similar to yours in topic, theme, style, story, or audience. Publishers use recent comps to project an estimate to their sales team of how a book will sell, and the more recent and realistic a comp is, the easier it becomes for an editor to make an argument in favor of publishing your book. Comps that are too old, or too aspirational, are usually ignored.

In other words, *Anna Karenina* is not a more worthwhile reference point than *Crazy Rich Asians*. In fact, a comp's function is even more commercial than artistic, so convincing your reader that your work has *Crazy Rich Asians*'s commercial viability is far more valuable than convincing them that it contains Tolstoy-level artistic genius.

So the question to ask yourself here is not "What titles are going to make this agent think I'm smart?" but rather "What are the stories that made me want to be a writer, and to write this story; what are the stories that hover over this one?"

I think it's savvy to include three comps, and to diversify them in terms of commercial viability, artistic credibility, and author. A strong comp assemblage, for example, might be one bestseller from within the last five years, one cult favorite from fifteen years ago, and one classic of literature. "This book is Glennon Doyle's *Untamed* meets Kate Zambreno's *Heroines*, through the lens of Claudia Rankine's *Citizen*."

You can also mix genres, such as including two books and a film to describe your book, as long as you're clear about the genre of the work you're pitching. Back in the day, my first agent pitched my lesbian YA novel using two films and a TV show: "*Saved!* meets *The L Word* meets *8 Mile*."

Hearing Back from Agents

If you send a polished package and follow the agent's procedure (including counting silence after X weeks a pass, or following up after X weeks, per their guidelines), you should get at least *some* responses. I've gotten a response (even a rejection) from most people, though not everyone, whom I've queried. Agents literally don't eat if they don't find new talent and sell it, plus their job is to be relentless in following up, so they tend to be approachable, gregarious, and responsive.

If one of these distinguished agents offers you representation, congratulations! Now you have a few things to do.

Overall, **I do not recommend accepting an offer of representation at the very moment it's offered.** You can express excitement, gratitude, and a wish to speak more, but I would advise responding to a representation offer with something like "Wow, that's so exciting, thank you so much. I want to show respect to all the agents I've queried, so could I round up responses and get you a firm answer by the end of the week?" I have never heard a reputable agent balk at this kind of request.

During that interim, and before signing any contracts, I recommend a few other due-diligence steps.

First, I'm about to give you loads of information about the boilerplate contract that usually connects author to agent, so ask the agent in question to send one for your review. This is very important: **Reputable agents eat when their authors eat.** There is so little that is standardized in media and publishing, but **it is *extremely* standard in the industry for agents to take 15 percent of a book's domestic advance and 20 percent of any foreign, TV, or film sales.** Now you know to **look askance at any agent who asks you for bigger cuts or cash up front.** Much to my chagrin, there are literary scammers out there who will sell you a bill of goods like "Well, I'm putting a lot of front-end work into this, so I need you to pay me $5,000 to make that worthwhile." *No.* A reputable agent is staking their earning ability upon yours, so they should bring *you* money, not the other way around.

It bears mentioning that this same scam can hijack the publishing stage too; I take a harder line on this than some do, but to my mind, any publisher who requires an author to pay up-front money for publication is a **vanity publisher.** These are companies that were once developed to give self-important retired businessmen the opportunity to put their professional life story into print (think *Mad Men*'s Roger Sterling publishing *Sterling's Gold*) and that now promise authors the opportunity to get into publishing without doing the hard work of penetrating the industry the traditional way. An inescapable truth about vanity publishing is that it rewards those who can afford to pay for a perceived shortcut; an anecdotal one is that the writers who *have* put in the long, hard work of establishing their byline tend not to take these shortcutters seriously. In our digital age, I've seen start-ups enter this space with a lot of language around "disrupting" traditional publishing, or about elevating marginalized voices, promising upswing for the underdog. While plenty of legitimate complaints can be levied (and are levied in this book!) about traditional publishing's exclusionary practices, I contend that self-publishing is much more dignified than vanity publishing: A self-published author takes home the majority of her sales income while usually paying nothing or very little to access the distribution platform. But any "publisher" that asks to be paid a significant up-front sum by writers instead of paying writers is exploitative bullshit.

In addition to asking to review a boilerplate contract, I recommend that you conduct a thorough frisk of this prospective agent's reputation. First, ask the agent to refer you to at least two other authors they represent. Reach out to those authors and solicit phone calls, *not* emails, and ask your nosiest questions. People are, for good reason, more candid on the phone than in writing, and the information these fellow authors wouldn't put into an email is *exactly* the information you need.

I would also consider one additional layer of frisking: Ask the authors you speak to if they can refer you to anyone else this agent represents or has ever represented, and/or do some research on your own to connect with authors this agent didn't mention to you. Agents will understandably select references who they suspect are likely to say glowing things about them, but again, if there are nonglowing things out there about them, you want to know those too. You will feel *great* about signing with somebody who passes all of these stress tests with flying colors, and if they don't pass, well, that's valuable information too. An agent is your public representative who will interface with the other gatekeepers with the power to make or break your career, so it is absolutely appropriate to be inquisitive and selective about how they handle their business. They will *literally* be handling yours, so choose with care.

Some questions I recommend asking these first- and second-degree references:

- How is this agent's response time to emails, typically?
- When you were in the querying stage, how did you find this specific agent, and why did you sign with them? Or if the agent found the author: What work attracted the agent's attention, and how did they approach you?
- How involved is this agent editorially? Do they give you rounds of notes or solicit others to give you feedback?

- How has this agent responded when you referred other author friends to them?
- What is the greatest thing this agent has ever done for you?
- Have you and this agent ever had a conflict? How did you navigate it?
- Is there anyone else you'd recommend I speak to?

There are no right or wrong answers to these questions, strictly speaking, but they should give you enough intel to determine if this agent suits your preferences. If I were to run down this list and evaluate my wonderful agents, Amanda Orozco and Brenna English-Loeb, I would tell someone querying them:

Amanda and Brenna respond promptly to emails, which I appreciate so much, and I also notice that all their written communications are composed in clean, beautiful prose. I found them because they were representing other talent I deeply admired, because they clearly liked and understood academics, and because a friend had delivered glowing reports on Amanda. They aren't tremendously involved editorially, and that's fine with me. They have responded warmly to all of my referrals whether they've signed the author or not. They sold a book for me within six months of signing with them, for a dollar amount larger than any other single-project contract I've ever signed. We have never had a conflict, and I can refer you to three other authors who would say equally glowing things about them.

My dream for you, dear reader, is to sign with an agent who is *that* easy to praise.

Of course, it may happen that you don't get a representation offer from your first three to five queries. And this is *fine.* I promise. Writing careers are built on stamina and dedication, not instant gratification. It may take some time but keep sending out the queries.

It may happen that you receive a pass from one specific agent but remain interested in other agents who work at their same agency. Some agencies discourage querying multiple agents at the same agency simultaneously (and will say so on their website), but pitching a different agent at a later date is generally fine. Just read the agency's submission guidelines carefully.

Some last notes on agent searches:

It's worth knowing that even if you sign with a literary agent, agents do not typically negotiate freelance, short-form assignments for you. Agents will assist you with negotiating book contracts, but you'll still handle 99 percent of your freelance editorial assignment contracts yourself. Very rarely, with a really big-deal publication such as a six-thousand-word feature in *Granta,* or a *GQ* cover story, your agent may get involved, but this is more the exception than the rule.

Even if you write in multiple genres, as I do, it's worthwhile to have one agent, or one team of agents, representing as many of your genres as possible. This helps ensure that your books are properly published and their in-print status maintained, inquiries about film or foreign rights to your books are handled effectively, your contracts are consistent, and most important, that you benefit from a unified publishing strategy. If, for example, you're published by a Big Publisher for your adult books, you may want to use that publishing relationship for your next YA novel and publish with one of Big Publisher's children's divisions—and it's helpful to have one agent directing communication between all imprints. Agents are also necessarily territorial, so it's ideal to make as few of them coordinate with each other as possible.

The one caveat I'll make on genre and representation is that if you write both screenplays and prose, you'll probably have one film/TV agent and one literary agent—sometimes they work at different divisions of the same agency, but not always.

Amicable breakups happen between authors and agents all the time. I basically lost an agent every time I added a genre until I signed with agents who were explicitly psyched about my multigenre tendencies. Agent contracts include some kind of at-will termination, which means you can end the relationship at any time. Some of them may specify a medium you have to use to terminate (such as written notification). If you're initiating the severance, just keep it simple: Write an email in which you thank them for their work and say you've decided to move on. If you're taking with you to the next agent an unsold manuscript that's already been out on submission, politely ask your outgoing agent to provide you with a list of their previous submissions: the editors the agent sent the manuscript to, the submission dates, and whether the editors passed or didn't respond.

CONTESTS: WORTH IT OR SKIP IT?

Should I submit my manuscript to contests or open reading periods that don't require agented submissions? Should I pay a submission fee?

Short answer: sometimes, but not most of the time.

Longer answer: I studied poetry in my MFA, and because poetry makes zero dollars for capitalism, the few poets who get book deals sometimes do so through first-book contests. In the absence of a better idea of how to get someone to publish my book of poems, I submitted my manuscript to a zillion first-book contests. A lot of those contests had ten- to twenty-five-dollar "reading fees."

I really wish I had all that money back. I got my book of poetry published when one of my friends decided to start a poetry press, meaning that buying my friends drinks at the college bar where I worked was literally a better investment in my career than spending twenty-five dollars on a first-book contest was.

Reading fees exist for contests in other genres too, and while many people argue that they are a necessary evil for funding small literary operations, I object to them. With some exceptions—big fellowships/grants/residencies, very reputable and established contests—I don't think you should pay people to read your work. Moreover, no matter how reputable or established the contest, submitting to it almost always means that your work will end up in a slush pile triaged by an intern and then something like twenty of one thousand entries will be passed on to the famous contest judges, so submitting to a contest does not usually lead to your work being given the best possible consideration.

Yes, great work stands out. But my point is just that submitting to a contest (especially with a full manuscript) means that you will be one in a thousand, while targeting a pitch gives you the opportunity to demonstrate to an editor or agent that you deserve their closest consideration because you have already given them yours.

Reading periods and/or contests also usually result in cookie-cutter book deals: For example, if your manuscript is selected, you'll receive a $2,000 advance and publication of your book. That may sound like a lot of money, but agents can negotiate for more. Agents have relationships with editors, so you're not just sitting in a slush pile hoping to be picked. A good agent will handpick a list of editors to submit your work to, based on their relationships and knowledge of those editors' tastes. Again, much less languishing in the slush pile.

Writing Your Story Synopses

Just as you did with your author bio, I recommend having short, medium, and long descriptions of your long-form project on hand—it's useful to be able to **describe your project in one sentence, one paragraph, and one page.** This ability is relevant to you both in the practice of pitching and in the craft of writing itself—whenever I have to write a project description, I writhe in self-loathing and hate it and avoid it, and inevitably, when it's done, I have a clearer sense of my priorities as a writer.

You'll use the short (one-sentence) and medium (one-paragraph) synopses for the majority of opportunities; the medium-length synopsis, for example, forms the substance of your query letter. Your long one-page synopsis may occasionally be requested by a residency, grant, fellowship, or writers' lab application, but this one-pager will be most relevant to your eventual book proposal, which I'll cover in the next chapter.

All of these synopses have three primary objectives: to grab the reader's attention, to invite the reader into your story's world, and to introduce your main characters and conflicts. Let me also note that this synopsis digest applies to fiction just a bit more directly than nonfiction; I will cover the craft of the nonfiction book proposal in greater detail in the next chapter.

The One-Line Synopsis

Your query letter, or any other description of your long work—a fellowship/residency application, for example—may incorporate both a broader, plot-forward, medium-length synopsis and a kicker of a one-line project description.

In my experience, the one-line description of your project arrives late in the game: once you've already talked and written about your project a lot, gotten a fair amount of feedback on it, and know it really, really well. The long synopsis is what you write when you're still figuring out what your book is about. The one-line synopsis is what you say when you know your book as well as a member of your family.

By the time I was done writing my YA novel *Sister Mischief* and was preparing to release it into the world, I'd been forced to have enough conversations, both professional and casual, about the book that I developed a one-line description of it just to save time: "What's my book about? My book is the world's first interracial gay hip-hop love story for teens."

This began as a pretty tongue-in-cheek description, way better suited to colloquial cocktail conversation than the formal language of applications or jacket copy, but, over time, I found it usually made people laugh, raised their eyebrows, or at least got them interested. Even if they were horrified, they were usually interested. (This is not an uncommon response to me in general.)

If I were to diagram the sentence of my one-line *Sister Mischief* pitch, I'd note how it does the following in no more than ten words:

- Makes the project sound unique and exciting ("the world's first").
- Clearly articulates the project's audience ("for teens").
- Gives a quick gloss of the story's tone, characters, world, and plot ("interracial gay hip-hop love story").

It's hard for me to give you a procedural step-by-step for the one-line project description, because I really do think that it's something you arrive at organically over time, once the idea of your project has moved through many drafts to something more polished and readier to be out in the world. Once a book is about to be published and you really can't change anything else about it, the idea of it becomes a more fixed point and thus easier to describe.

All that said, here are a few tips and tricks to consider as you hunt for your hole in one:

- What is the single most important thing about your book? What was the kernel of the idea that wouldn't leave you alone that eventually became your story?
- In what way is your book the "world's first"?
- How does your book combine several elements in an unexpected way ("interracial gay hip-hop love story")?
- What is the central question of your story? In your long or medium synopsis, you may provide some information about how the question is answered, but the question itself can tell a story in your one-liner.

And here are a few examples of what I think are bomb-dropping one-liners:

The story of two girls and the feral year that will cost one her life, and define the other's for decades, Julie Buntin's *Marlena* is an unforgettable look at the people who shape us beyond reason and the ways it might be possible to pull oneself back from the brink.

What does it mean to lose your roots—within your culture, within your family—and what happens when you find them? (Nicole Chung's *All You Can Ever Know*)

Combining memoir with powerful analysis and cultural commentary, Sarah Smarsh's *Heartland* is an uncompromising look at class, identity, and the particular perils of having less in a country known for its excess.

You don't have a self until you have a secret. (Megan Abbott's *Give Me Your Hand*)

The Medium-Length Synopsis

Ironically, I am about to spend several paragraphs describing everything that should go into this single paragraph: Let this serve as a reminder that this material is important and ought to travel through multiple drafts.

A medium-length synopsis in a great query letter immediately grabs the reader's attention with a dramatic, memorable opening paragraph. This paragraph introduces your main character's central conflict and ends with one thesis sentence that encapsulates the primary questions/concerns of your project. **Focus most heavily on plot propulsion:** *What happens* **over the arc of your story, and what primary plot points motivate and signpost this action?** What are your story's main conflicts, and how are they negotiated? Most long-form stories unfold over three or four acts; give each act one to two sentences, roughly. Convince the reader that the character and plot action of your story makes sense, feels inevitable, and unfolds suspensefully. Create a sense of mounting stakes as the plot unfolds: What is the barbed wire in which your primary actors entangle themselves, and how does their furious effort to escape only entangle them further? What or who depends on this effort, what is the deadline, and what will happen if your hero/ine doesn't achieve their goal?

Either reveal the conclusion—the third act—of the story in a compelling, satisfying way, or ask very intriguing, suspenseful questions that tease the story's conclusion: "After X TOTALLY BANANAS PLOT DEVELOPMENT results in Y SIGNIFICANT CHANGE FOR YOUR CHARACTER, how will she navigate the darkness that lies ahead?"

Provide fresh, evocative descriptions of your main **characters,** including key supporting characters, and their journeys through the story. Use your major conflicts and plot events to illustrate who your main characters are. What are they up against? How do they react to each other and their surroundings? What choices do they make, and what choices are made for them? Most important, how do they change?

You'll also want to bring the reader into the **world** of the story. Painting a vivid picture of your story's era, geographical location, atmosphere, structure, and style will invite your reader into this world. Where and when does your story take place, and how does it feel to be there?

Finally, **make a bold, grand statement about the intent of your work.** "A sweeping, intimate dive into the high drama of pregnancy, birth, and new motherhood" is way more interesting than "A glimpse of what it means to be a new mother." Ask the big questions of your book at the end of this synopsis: Again, what are the stakes of this story? What makes it urgent, necessary, and unique? "Dying, what story would you tell?"

Here are a few **examples** of wonderful, vivid medium-length synopses from my friend and professional wellness consultant Adrian Van Young.

For his novel *Shadows in Summerland* (this is technically a two-paragraph synopsis, but we'll still call it medium-length):

Boston, 1859. A nation on the brink of war. Confidence men prowl the streets for fresh marks, and mediums swindle the newly bereaved. Into this world of illusion and intrigue comes William Mumler, a photographic prodigy and criminal jeweler, who seeks to grasp his own main chance by photographing spirits for Boston's elite. The key to his venture: a young girl named Hannah who sees and manifests the dead. Thus begins a partnership between her and Mumler as strange and perverse as it is undefined— a shifting world of light and shade where nothing is quite what it seems at first glance.

Shadows in Summerland is a soaring and resplendently Gothic novel spanning three decades and narrated in nineteenth-century vernacular by five different first-person voices. It is not only a panoramic character study, but a grand-scale meditation on mid-nineteenth-century America. The novel is as much a paean to the Golden Age ghost stories of Edith Wharton and Henry James as it is a companion piece to the postmodern historical novels of Peter Carey, John Wray, and Sarah Waters, with a little steampunk all its own.

And for his short story collection *The Man Who Noticed Everything:*

Ruined dandies, obsessive loners, young men at loose ends, and more than a few unaffiliated supernatural entities navigate with varying degrees of success the literal and figurative labyrinths of Adrian Van Young's neo-Gothic universe. A chicken-hawk tobacco farmer in Depression-era rural

Georgia welcomes a dangerous drifter into his diminished circle of trust. An amnesiac burn-victim hoping to escape his dubious past forges a series of ragged connections with the occupants of a small town after joining a crew of day laborers hired to exhume a graveyard on a rich man's property. A lovesick son of the South pursues an unknown nemesis through Civil War–era Virginia, attended by three grotesque spirits who prognosticate in riddles on the outcome of his quest. A man so quintessentially average-looking that he cannot be perceived by others finds himself the subject of a macabre plot that musters in the tunnels of the New York City subway system.

Here's another one-paragraph synopsis I love, for Angie Thomas's *The Hate U Give:*

Sixteen-year-old Starr Carter navigates between the poverty-stricken neighborhood she has grown up in and the upper-crust suburban prep school she attends. Her life is upended when she is the sole witness to a police officer shooting her best friend, Khalil, who turns out to have been unarmed during the confrontation—but may or may not have been a drug dealer. As Starr finds herself even more torn between the two vastly different worlds she inhabits, she also has to contend with speaking her truth and, in the process, trying to stay alive herself.

And for another terrific YA novel, Emily Horner's *A Love Story Starring My Dead Best Friend* (I'd also call that title itself a near-perfect one-line synopsis):

For months, Cass has heard her best friend, Julia, whisper about a secret project. When Julia dies in a car accident, her drama friends decide to bring the project, a musical called *Totally Sweet Ninja Death Squad,* to fruition. But Cass isn't a drama person. She can't take a summer of painting sets, and she won't spend long hours with Heather, the girl who made her miserable all through middle school and has somehow landed the leading role. So Cass takes off. In alternating chapters, she spends the first part of summer on a cross-country bike trip and the rest swallowing her pride, making props, and, of all things, falling for Heather. This is a story of the breadth of love. Of the depth of friendship. And of the most hilarious musical one quiet suburb has ever seen.

Here's the one-paragraph description of my film *Farah Goes Bang:*

The road-trip comedy of *Farah Goes Bang* follows a woman in her twenties, Farah Mahtab, who tries to lose her virginity while campaigning across America for presidential candidate John Kerry in 2004. Farah and her friends K.J. and Roopa follow the campaign trail across historic Route 66 on their way to Ohio, the central battleground state of 2004, seizing control of this charged moment in their lives and the life of their country. Roopa aspires to a job in politics, K.J. brawls through a personal motivation to end the war in Iraq, and Farah struggles to locate not just her desirability, but her desire. We know how the election turns out—but will Farah meet her personal goal for their American odyssey?

The Long, One-Page Synopsis

This is the synopsis that will see the least light of day, but that doesn't make it any less important. You may use a one-page description of your story for a big application, but most of the time, its primary venue is the book proposal. Read on to the next chapter for my detailed thoughts on book proposals, including their detailed summaries!

ASSIGNMENT

- Write **short** (one to two lines) and **medium** (one paragraph) **project descriptions** of the novel, story/essay collection, memoir, or screenplay I know you're working on.
- Using your medium project description as a springboard, **write a draft query letter** to one of the agents you targeted during your networking efforts. Either incorporate the main highlights of your author bio into the letter itself or append your medium/long author bio to the bottom of your query letter. Include the rough page/word count of your manuscript, a few comps, and why you selected this particular agent.
- Especially if querying agents is an immediate goal for you, keep scanning acknowledgments pages and author websites, and **narrow in on three to five agents you'd like to query.** Start tailoring individual query letters to those agents' lists and interests.
- Build a **submissions tracker for your agent queries**—you can even add this as a tab in the submissions tracker you already built for your short-form submissions. Even if you're not ready to send out any queries yet, start keeping track of agents of interest here.

CHAPTER 6

Your Book's Business Plan

The Book Proposal

A crucial and criminally underdiscussed element of selling a book, particularly a work of nonfiction, is the **book proposal,** which is the document your agent will use to present your work to editors. While the quality of your writing will be influential in gaining editorial interest in your book, it's the way you package your work's marketability that will convince an editor that a hungry audience will buy your work. The clarity of the road map you draw between book and audience in your proposal will determine how fast and for how much your book sells.

A book proposal is a business document. The business is literature and publishing, yes, but an effective book proposal will demonstrate a direct connection between your words and your audience's dollars. It is an outline of a book's relationship to the bottom line. **The proposal is, in essence, your book's business plan.** The primary elements it will include are several chapters of your book, your agent's information, some marketing information, and some history of your previous work. Never fear: I'm about to shepherd you in immense detail through all of those elements and more.

But before that, I want you to tattoo one shimmering, abiding principle on your brain: **Your book proposal is a vehicle to make it as easy as possible for an editor to say yes.** A great book proposal conveys: "Hi there, not only am I a talented, experienced, hellaciously dedicated writer, but here are four books demonstrably similar to mine that sold well, here's the multipronged public platform I've been cultivating for years, here is the reputable agent who's staked her ability to eat on my ability to produce, here's a clear strategy for continuing to expand my target audience, and here is my gripping, convincing argument for why this book urgently needs to exist."

To quote my friend Emily Best, writer, director, and CEO of film crowdfunding platform Seed&Spark, a great pitch answers four questions in the most compelling, emotionally connective, creative way possible:

- Why me?
- Why this?
- Why now?
- And why do we need you involved?

So, let's break it down: here is your bespoke guided tour to writing book proposals that *sell*.

Your Opening Pages

Never fudge the first page. Just as I exhorted you to pay close attention to the subject line of your pitch email to a magazine editor, so too will I implore you to **make your cover page attractive and**

attention-grabbing. Obviously, this page should include the book's title and your name (or pen name). If you have graphic-design skills, this is absolutely a place to flex them. If you, like me, are overdeveloped in textual skill and grossly underdeveloped in everything else, then recruiting a graphic designer to beautify your document can be a fantastic idea. It should be intentionally designed; purposefully connected to the work; and vividly, clearly presented. The first page is your first impression, so make one that conveys care.

Your Agent's Information

Another deceptively simple element! If you're at the point of creating a book proposal, you've likely already done the work of querying agents and signing with one you love. In that scenario, your agent may help you assemble your book proposal, as mine did, and their name and contact information will simply appear on the second page of the proposal. While querying, use this image to gauge how comfortable you are with an agent representing your work: Do you like and trust them enough to emblazon their name on your most prized work?

I do want to mention, also, that **you can use a book proposal to approach agents.** The initial query process will go as I outlined in the previous chapter: You'll craft an excellent, plot-forward query letter, attach it to a polished opening chapter, and send that as your first outreach. Then, when the agent requests your full manuscript, you can send them that manuscript already framed in a killer proposal. (Note: For nonfiction, it's fine for the proposal to consist of several chapters of an unfinished manuscript; in fiction, especially debut fiction, you put yourself in the strongest position with a proposal attached to a finished manuscript.)

This is an extra-credit strategy, because you certainly *can* send agents a finished manuscript that's not yet packaged into a proposal; I and many others have successfully done this. But agents are gatekeepers just as editors are, and all gatekeepers love an achiever who understands and can address the bottom line. Your call.

A Book Overview

The first text entry of significant volume in your proposal will be **a tight, propulsive summary of the book you're proposing. Speak directly and emphatically to the four core pitch questions: Why me, why this, why now, and why do I need you involved?**

If you're agented, the overview is an area where having already put quality work into your query materials will be a huge benefit: Now you have a ton of practice in summarizing your book. My agents imported lots of text for this book proposal's overview from my initial query letter, which felt gratifying, given the amount of work I'd invested into that letter.

A compelling overview, in about one page, provides a convincing answer to this question: What gaping hole in the market does this book fill, and why are you the ideally qualified thinker to fill it? In what way did you write the book you needed the most, and who else needs it?

As in general pitch structure, the arc of this argument generally opens with what the reader might already know about this topic, proceeds into some things about this topic that might surprise the reader, and makes it obvious why the reader should care about the topic. All of this should convey a sense of **mission:** Your book will help people in a crucial way, so getting it into those people's hands is a matter of proportional urgency.

To give you a concrete example, here's how my agents Amanda and Brenna and I overviewed the book you're currently reading:

The art of writing has been taught and studied in almost every imaginable form. Writers learn the craft through an MFA, or through the hundreds of books, essays, YouTube tutorials, TED Talks, and MasterClass courses on the subject. But what about the art of getting paid for your labor? Who teaches writers to wield their persuasive storytelling abilities to market themselves—and more crucially, to make a living?

Throughout six years of writing education at Ivy League universities, including an almost $100,000 MFA from one of the most "prestigious" writing programs in the country, not one professor taught Laura Goode how to pitch, publish, or get paid for her writing. This egregious gap in graduate humanities pedagogy reflects how gatekept the literary community remains and reveals the urgent need for collective bargaining power among writers, which can coalesce only from the free and promiscuous sharing of information.

PITCH CRAFT is a craft book designed to guide writers through the business of selling their work. Its procedural stories, tips, and tricks dissect the process of pitching across genres, demystifying the publishing and media sectors. Its lessons emerge from the professional and lived experience of a lifelong writer—one who has published two books; has held full-time reporting jobs; has written, produced, funded, and distributed an independent film; has worked with two literary agents and a film agent; has written for a vibrant bouquet of magazines; has taught the craft of writing everywhere from maximum-security prisons to elementary school classrooms; and now serves as Stanford University's resident expert on the business of writing.

In each chapter, readers dive into a distinct element of pitching. Readers will learn procedures to construct effective author bios and websites, to connect strategically with editors and agents, to deploy a reliable template for writing pitches and query letters, and to strengthen their negotiating and self-advocacy. The book parses the pros and cons of MFA programs, providing an insider's opinion on the age-old question, "Should I go to graduate school?" Interspersed among direct instruction and Q&A-style teachings are stories of professional successes and failures. Through these reflections, Laura Goode examines the fraught relationship between writing and capitalism, encouraging readers to choose their own paths and claim their own definitions of what it means to be a writer. In analyzing the psychologies of fear and anxiety, this book answers the most frequently asked pitching questions, honors the vulnerability of the reader, and disarms anxiety with actionable strategies. Chapter assignments encourage readers to set concrete goals toward their writing aspirations, and the book's templates and real-world examples arm them with the required knowledge to achieve them. PITCH CRAFT presents a book-length argument that a great pitch is simply a performance of confidence: With the right information, you can present a compelling argument for your work no matter how terrified or underqualified you may feel.

And readers might just take away an understanding of how this performance of confidence can extend beyond writing in one's life.

After reading PITCH CRAFT, readers can expect to have a finished pitch in hand, and a connection to the book's community of writers intent on making a literary career more accessible and sustainable. Laura expects the full manuscript will be ready by Summer 2024 and will be approximately 60,000 words.

As you can see, this overview delivers "why this" (nobody else teaches writers how to sell their work), "why me" (I have professional experience in multiple genres of writing, and a large university with a recognizable name regards me as an expert in this material), and "why do I need you involved" (publishing this material means making it available to anyone with fifteen bucks or a library card, which enhances writers' ability to bargain collectively).

I will also tell you candidly that I don't think this pitch explicitly answers "why now" beyond referring to the "urgent" need for collective bargaining power, and that as I pulled this excerpt, I fixed one lingering typo that I will never reveal. And then the copyeditors fixed two more. I mention these facts to defang perfectionism: There is no such thing as a perfect pitch, and this imperfect one sold. Fortune favors the bold.

Your Author Bio

No need to belabor this point: If you've read this far, you've already collected all my best tips for writing author bios. The book proposal is a venue for your **long author bio, roughly one page.** Go *hard* on this one. Your hardest.

Your Publicity and Marketing Platform

After the proposal has introduced you, your representation, and the book to the reader, it should devote several pages of well-researched ammunition to your platform as an author, including **a definition of your target audience, how your book answers a need of that audience, and how you will help the publisher reach those readers.** You'll want to feature all possible prongs of your platform, including but not limited to the following.

Previous Publications

First, demonstrate that you already *have* an audience: Provide a collection of links to your best published work. Link directly to the publication if the story is still live; if it was a print story, or if the website and its archive have gone to the big library in the sky, the Wayback Machine and PDFs hosted on your personal website can help. (Please implement a regular practice of saving PDFs of your stories; I save my recent clips every winter break.) Favor the biggest-name publications and the stories you're proudest to present. If any of these bylines went viral, make sure to mention that, ideally with numbers. If you have juicy screenshots of complimentary tweets, particularly from recognizable people, consider throwing one or two of those in too.

Multimedia and Other Creative Experience

Do you have any previous creative experience that doesn't fit neatly under "publications"? This is where you put it. Maybe you wrote and produced a one-act play. Maybe you have a podcast. Maybe you've edited more than ten thousand Wikipedia articles. Maybe you published a chapbook with a small poetry press and you'd rather feature it here than as one little link under "previous publications." Podcasts, newsletters, eclectic awards, significant projects, charming obsessions—put them here.

Speaking Engagements

Particularly for nonfiction authors, have you ever been invited to speak about your book topic? Have you ever been interviewed on someone else's podcast about it? Participated in a panel? Given a keynote, even for an audience of eight people? Taught a class on your topic? Guest-appeared in someone else's class? Read your work at Litquake? Become the go-to emcee for all the events your favorite nonprofit holds? Mention it all.

Another note here: When describing your speaking experience, or any other experience that you think might benefit from more context, don't be afraid to tell a story. Many of us arrive at the story we most need to tell after facing some kind of adversity or obstacle, so if this story is important to you because it was hard-won, let the reader in on that struggle.

To illustrate what I mean, here's how I wrote about "Speaking Engagements" in the proposal for this book:

In 2016, out of churning resentment for everything she hadn't been taught in her MFA program, Laura designed a class called "How to Pitch Anything," which ran for seven sessions online with Catapult and became one of its most popular courses for writers. In 2017, one of her former Catapult students invited her to guest-speak to graduate students on pitching and publishing. The class that resulted from this, "Pitching and Publishing for Popular Media," has since become a cornerstone of Stanford's emergent programming on the public humanities. To date, her pitching and publishing curricula have served 147 students and produced 96 student publications at Stanford. Now regarded as one of the university's resident experts in the business of literature, Laura has been frequently invited beyond her home departments of English and feminist, gender, and sexuality studies to guest-lecture for Stanford's Queer Learning Initiative, Clayman Institute for Gender Research, McCoy Family Center for Ethics in Society, Center for Comparative Studies in Race & Ethnicity, and master's in journalism program, and at the University of Southern California.

Social Media

Whether we like it or not—and as I write this in 2024, I sit decidedly in the "not" camp—social media still represents an important prong of platform and publicity. While sizable followings tend to matter more to nonfiction and film/TV projects than they do to fiction and poetry, they do matter. Are you a gregarious person who can make friends with strangers? Do you have a sharp intuition for self-presentation? Are you deft with a punchline? Are you smart and engaging? Social media can put all these virtues on display.

Obviously, the gatekeepers like big numbers in follower counts. A **robust following** on any major platform can help you: X/Twitter, Instagram, Substack, TikTok, YouTube. So it may serve you to put some time into building a following on one of those places. Play to your talents, prepare for some disappointment, don't buy bots, and always prioritize your mental health.

However, because I've found that quantitative anxiety over not having enough followers can quickly bloom into panic attacks, I also want to address some qualitative things that matter about social media presence. Rest assured that gatekeepers will take these elements into consideration just as they do follower counts.

The first is **consistency.** By no means do you have to post thirty times a day. I tend to heart and reply to many more posts than I originate myself. But it is glaringly obvious to those of us who hang around the water cooler of online discourse when people create a social media account fifteen minutes before releasing a book announcement, when their only posts are self-promoting, or when those posts get intrusive. I *hate* being mass-tagged in anything, and that strategy is likelier to make me block a person than to buy their book. Pick a platform that doesn't give you hives and engage there in an ongoing way.

Next is **civility and integrity.** Don't get it twisted: I am *not* saying you should never engage in political discourse, offer an opinion, or even get a little salty. The most cursory glance at my body of public work would make such counsel ridiculous. But in addition to looking at follower count, gatekeepers also look at online *conduct* when making decisions. It matters if a stranger looking at your recent posts sees a wild abundance of support for other authors and a total absence of punching down at less powerful people. Basically, don't be a dick online, and don't be a dick offline either. There exists a persistent misconception that if you're talented beyond all reason, you can treat people badly, but by contrast, many of the most successful people I've ever known have also been the most delightful. Read how feature writers describe Tom Hanks's personal conduct and aim for that.

Finally, we have **voice and originality.** When someone reads your tweets or posts, does a human with relatively coherent interests, opinions, and personality appear? Your social media presence should demonstrate that you can generate original thoughts, rather than only reposting from others in a generic way, which makes you indistinguishable from a bot. Social media is a great place to put your weirdest (legal) obsessions on display. Quote your favorite authors. Ship your favorite TV couples. Crack a joke. We jumped the shark on "be yourself" around the time we started packaging ourselves into one-inch avatars, but be *somebody.*

Endorsements

Just like every other industry in America's stage play of meritocracy, publishing and media are powered by the fuel of Who You Know. Much as I hope that the publication of this book will end literary nepotism and cronyism forever by distributing "insider" information widely, we're not there yet. These forces still have influence, and they are the primary reason why I've spent so much page space encouraging you to Build. Your. Network. There is more than one way to build a network, and there are many, many people within it who are worth knowing. But very few people sell a book without demonstrating that its author already has the support of some people of influence.

Under "endorsements," you're going to list the names of all of the most famous, semifamous, or at minimum published people to whom you've ever been connected, in any capacity. The list you're assembling conveys, "Here are all the accomplished people I would be comfortable asking for a blurb." It does *not* require that you have already committed every single one of these people to writing a blurb. Let me also quell panic by reassuring you that *connected* can be interpreted *very* loosely here. You are allowed to include under "endorsements" people you've met once, or with whom you're distantly acquainted. Many people include their professors, their author friends, or other authors represented by their agency. Once you move from book proposal endorsements to book cover blurbs, many authors solicit blurbs from other authors published by their publisher. While I stand behind all my advice to put some back into building your network, please *do not* feel as if you have to know fifteen people who have been on the cover of *Vanity Fair*, or even authored cover stories for *Vanity Fair*, just to assemble a list of endorsements.

BLURBS

Within the industry, we use the term *blurb* to denote the one to two lines of florid compliments by another author that appear on a book cover. Every time you see one of those compliments, picture the groveling email that the book's sweaty-handed author or agent wrote to the more famous author begging for it. Neither the famous nor the unfamous love this process, but compliments from recognizable names are still effective in grabbing reader attention.

Once you get to the point of actually requesting blurbs, you are allowed to request from someone whose reading you attended, or even someone you've never met whose work you revere (though I wouldn't recommend listing these people under "endorsements").

Of course, that author is equally allowed to decline your request, and your request should gracefully and explicitly acknowledge that possibility. Since we're only talking about endorsements for the purpose of the book proposal here, we'll get into gorier detail about how to ask for blurbs for your imminently forthcoming book in the next chapter.

The point is: **This list of endorsements should include anyone who you have *any* reason to believe is even *fractionally* likely to praise your book.** My most recent endorsements list included a range from obvious picks (my closest friends) to some hugely ambitious ones (heroines of mine that I had never met). Again, go hard.

Comp Titles

We already covered how to select comps (page 92): You want to prioritize titles that sold well in the recent past (up to five years ago), and working with an ideal list of three or four comps, you might choose one award winner that reflects your artistic style and two bestsellers that represent the huge audience for this kind of work.

You will impress editors by making these comps *realistic*. Editors sigh when they read pitches claiming this book is the next *Harry Potter, Eat Pray Love,* or *Wild*. Your comps should demonstrate your voracious reading and familiarity with the market as well as the themes of your book.

The comps you choose for your agent query letter may be different from the comps you choose for your book proposal, particularly if you end up working with a smart agent who has sharp insights about what comps will best position your book.

What's important is that you include the following information for your comps: title, author, publication date, publisher, retail price, and number of copies sold. (Usually your agent can source this sales information from an industry insider tool such as Book-Scan.) You might also include, if relevant, bestseller rankings; whether the book was published in hardcover, paperback, or both; and number of pages.

Book Content

Once you've planted your marketing flag in the ground, the proposal pivots toward captivating its reader with actual selections from your glorious book.

Table of Contents

You'll open this section with a simple element: a brief, numbered, titled list of all the book chapters in your proposal. Make it pretty.

Next is an extended, or annotated, table of contents (TOC), where you'll spend more time and page space. Here you want to devote a **tight-but-substantial paragraph to summarizing each chapter.** In a procedural, cumulative way, **invite the reader on a walking tour of each chapter:** its main points, its connections to the sense of mission you established in your overview, its most striking facts or figures. A good agent will be likely to help you with the extended TOC, but you should plan to spend a significant amount of time polishing each chapter summary to optimal specificity and dazzle.

Again: If you've done a thorough job summarizing your book for your agent query letter, you've already generated a great starting place for this asset. And just as I recommended for that query, the longer chapter summaries in your annotated TOC should convey a sensation of urgency, inevitability, and mounting stakes.

Overall, I believe that **any act of summarizing should travel through multiple drafts.** As noted, you will commit acts of summarizing at many different stages: in your query letter, in your book proposal, in eighteen different applications for residencies and grants, and ultimately on your book's cover, in interviews about your book, and in endless party conversations. This extended TOC is probably the most extensive act of summarizing you will commit, so give it the time and attention it deserves.

Sample Chapters

At the glowing heart of your proposal, of course, will be several chapters of your most sterling writing work. For an unfinished book, a proposal includes five to ten chapters, somewhere in the neighborhood of 50 to 150 pages—and the proposal should also gesture, probably in the overview or annotated TOC, toward how and when you plan to finish the book, and roughly how many words the anticipated finished product will be.

There is really no overstating how important it is that these sample chapters be thoroughly proofed, refined through several drafts and readers, and work that you are deeply proud to present. All writers wrestle with feelings of self-doubt, and I personally never find my writing more mediocre than in the moments right before or right after I send it to a gatekeeper. But if *you* are not still genuinely excited about this work, you will never persuade anyone else to be enthusiastic about it either. I've said it one hundred different ways, and I will say it again: These gatekeepers will look at your manuscript only once, so take whatever time you need to be sure you're presenting your best work. Many, many more people meet disappointment by sending pages out too early than too late.

Here is a stripped-down template of the whole book proposal so you can track the process.

OPENING PAGES
(THREE TO FIVE PAGES)

- Gorgeous cover page: book's title and your (pen) name
- Agent name(s) and contact info
- Overview: why the world needs this book in about one gripping page
- Author bio: go hard

PUBLICITY AND MARKETING
(THREE TO FIVE PAGES)

- Selected published writing: your best and brightest by-lines
- Multimedia and other creative experience: your coolest projects that didn't fit under selected published writing, like podcasts or performances
- Speaking engagements
- Social media
- Endorsements
- Comp titles (three or four realistic choices)

BOOK CONTENT
(FIFTY TO ONE HUNDRED PAGES)

- Brief TOC
- Extended TOC
- Sample chapters

My final word on book proposals: A great proposal takes *time* to generate. Once, a very talented undergraduate writer excitedly wrote to me that she had just met a promising editor who requested her manuscript. She understandably wanted to strike while the iron was hot, so could I send her my best tips and tricks for completing her book proposal between Friday and Monday?

This expected pace, I told my wonderfully bright and motivated student, is not one that respects the *years* of work you have put into becoming a writer with a full draft that intrigues an editor. So please honor the depth of work you've poured into your book by devoting a proportional amount of attention to your proposal. Just as your book is, your proposal is a vehicle for demonstrating your creativity, ingenuity, professionalism, and talent. Take the time to make it shine.

CHAPTER 7

Bless and Release

The Book Promotion Phase

While writers spend an outsized proportion of life locked away with our own forced hallucinations, occasionally we do need to leave the cloister to share our work with the world. It often goes like this: You toil in solitary for years, eventually a good-news phone call arrives, and suddenly your book is about to be published. What on earth should a debut writer do now?

Book Tour Myth-Busting

When my first book, *Sister Mischief*, was about to be released, I knew I wanted to host events celebrating the book in multiple cities, and I fully expected my publisher would coordinate and fund a whole national tour. When I emailed the publicity department at Candlewick Press—a department consisting of one person—with this ambition, I received a gently worded response saying, in effect: Cute idea, honey, we'll give you $500.

Never easily deterred, I took the $500 and begged my parents for enough frequent flyer miles to cover three domestic flights. I tallied the metro areas where I had a free place to crash: New York, Boston, western Massachusetts, Chicago, Minneapolis, and Los Angeles. I booked budget flights and begged friends for interstitial rides. I doggedly networked my way to booksellers in each place: through friends, friends' moms, friends of friends. I acquired a Square so I could run sales myself and had books shipped to each destination. I found an event hall near my house in San Francisco that would rent me a large audio-equipped space for a song if I was willing to have my release party on a Thursday. From this process I learned how to select areas to visit, how to endear myself to booksellers, and what kinds of nonbookstore events to seek.

These were tremendously meaningful events for me, personally, and I wouldn't trade them for anything in the world. But now is the time when I must throw cold water on this nostalgia-tinged rhapsody.

None of these fun, emotionally significant events moved very many copies of my book. So what does?

Effective Book Promotion

For insights on book promotion, I turned to many sources, including certified expert Leigh Stein, an independent editor, founding denizen of the now-defunct, semisecret Binders Full of Women Writers group and author of the must-read newsletter *Attention Economy.* Leigh's five published books include the darkly hilarious novel *Self Care,* which she pitched as "*American Psycho* set in the *Goop* universe," so you *know* this woman knows a thing or two about sales language.

Leigh distilled one particularly valuable insight for me: the difference between *marketing* and *publicity.* "Publicity happens once, at launch, when your book is new. You get one shot," she explained.

"Marketing can happen for *years*. I'm still marketing *Self Care* four years after its publication."

To parse the distinction between marketing and publicity, it can also be helpful to understand the different roles of a marketer and a publicist. Publicists, for example, will write your book's press release and solicit press interest in the book through magazines, newspapers, radio, podcasts, TV, reviews, and the like. Also, publicists and their deep networks are often enormously helpful with coordinating events. Marketers focus more on objects, like influencer mailings and print collateral (postcards, stickers, bookmarks) for your promotion, as well as on digital assets such as banners, book trailers, and bookseller pages.

Another way to understand this difference is that marketing is actually something you can control—the message, the visuals, the storytelling—through "owned" channels such as your social media, newsletter, communities, and collaborators. By contrast, publicity is "earned," meaning that you pitch the book and story, but the channel for and specific take on your work are controlled by another media entity.

So everything we've detailed up to this point—your author bio, website, social media presence, individual pitches and publications, agent queries, and book proposal—are acts of *marketing*. Marketing is ongoing, multipronged, diffuse. It will happen for years leading up to your debut book's publication and for years succeeding it.

Great marketing and publicity around your book's publication will cultivate a first audience of readers—enthusiastic members of this first audience then become "book ambassadors" through word of mouth and personal recommendations. This is the holy grail of marketing: Research consistently shows that an organic recommendation from a friend is the #1 driver of product purchases. So a savvy marketing strategy will put resources toward pursuing a wildly enthusiastic first audience as a mode of pursuing the ultimate audience of millions.

Publicity is roughly a twelve-week hard sprint—six weeks leading up to your pub date and six weeks following it. This is stressful! It will take a lot out of you. So, while I think you should maximize all possible publicity opportunities within that twelve-week window, it's also helpful to remember that these twelve weeks, alone, will not determine the total market viability of your book.

Turn All Your Sales Language to Face the Reader

Great news: Most of marketing and publicity ultimately comes back to text, and you generate text professionally. But the biggest misconception writers often carry into their publication season, Leigh says, is the assumption that "someone down the line in publishing will figure out the pitch."

Leigh (and I) could not disagree with this assumption more. "*No. You* reverse-engineer the sale, starting with the query letter." Do not, do not, do *not* wait for anybody else to plan a sales strategy for you: This job absolutely starts with you.

In fact, I would argue that this reverse engineering begins even before the query letter! By now you have heard me exhort you to work *hard* on descriptive language around your book for many venues: your author bio, your author website, the bio that accompanies your story pitches, your agent query letter, and your book proposal. The through line that connects all these assets is that they are *cumulative.* Of the documents I just listed, the query letter will contain the most extensive summary. Remember: Any act of summarizing should travel through multiple drafts while you are still in the conceptualization stage, and the aforementioned twelve-week sprint period at publication is one of many reasons why.

Citing Ben Smith's book *Traffic*, Leigh notes that *BuzzFeed* identified exactly four motives that connect a reader with writing: The work is inspiring, motivating, entertaining, or educational. Readers don't buy your book to marvel at the fact that you've read Tolstoy, Dostoevsky, *and* Kafka—they buy your book to laugh, learn, cry, or ideally all three in three hundred pages or less.

So, by all means, make your reader think, but never allow that to come at the expense of making them *feel*—and this goes for marketing language as well as the contents of the book itself.

Booksellers shine at this reader-facing language. Think of the way "shelf-talkers" at your favorite bookstore describe a book:

- If you loved V, X, and Y books, you will *devour* Z book.
- If your favorite book at age twelve was A, then your favorite book at age thirty is destined to be B.
- Taut, funny, and page-turning, this debut essay collection is giving baby Queer Icon.
- I loved this novel about motherhood so much it made me forget to feed or bathe my children.

Netflix routinely kneecaps me with this kind of auto-generated description of my viewing tastes: For Fans of Female-Driven Cozy Murder Stories. For Fans of Moody International Lesbian Tragedies. For Educators Who Admit Espionage Fantasies in Therapy. For Professional Feminists Inexplicably Drawn to Mafia Cinema. As in stories, *conflict* and *surprise* are what make topical marketing language attention-grabbing.

Nourish this process with big, diverse, ongoingly evolving

combinations of words. What are the juiciest words that describe your work? Ask your friends: how would they describe your project? **Picture yourself as a besotted bookseller who's desperately trying to impress on a buyer the specific ways in which this book will surely change their life forever:** How would you convince them that it is inspiring, motivating, entertaining, or educational?

Collaborate with Your Publisher's Team

First and foremost, I advise you to treat anyone who works for your publisher, and in particular their publicity and marketing team, with the sparkling respect you would bestow on a partner. Recognize that these are underpaid, overworked people who would surely be making four times their salary in another job if they didn't love words and the people who generate them so damn much. Do not *ever* condescend to them, take them for granted, or treat them as adversaries. Recognize that people who are delightful to work with tend to work more than their opposites, and be delightful to *everyone* at your publishing house. As with all sectors of publishing, and the business world at large, you never know when today's assistant will be tomorrow's acquiring editor, so do your utmost to build a reputation of integrity.

This kind of delightful, respectful behavior should reflect that you appreciate the partnership this team is offering you: You respond promptly to emails, fill out their long questionnaires about your affiliations, engage their insights, and listen to them. It should also include a recognition that *your* **networks and contacts are much likelier to move copies than your publisher's lists**—this is what the long questionnaire is for. While I agree capitalism is a bummer, your book sales will rely in large part on your connections to brands, institutions, and other large networks. So on the eve of your book's release, you should be *very* prepared to serve up your contacts to your partners in publicity and marketing.

Note: It takes time and effort to curate networks. Remember when I advised you to start a newsletter *years* before ever publishing a book? To go to events in person, ask thoughtful questions, and make friends? To cultivate a like-minded community of writers, and to be generous with them in sharing your feedback and contacts? To say yes to opportunities that you don't fully understand when offered by interesting, trustworthy people? These are all actions that build a network. On the precipice of releasing a book, you will be tasked with activating this network in a *big* and *fast* way, so it literally pays to spend years of your prerelease life cultivating this network.

How to Ask for Blurbs

Our tour through book proposals gestured at the concept of "blurbs," the deeply fraught practice whereby an about-to-publish writer asks a more famous writer (or other professional, depending on your book's topic) to write a few complimentary lines for the book's cover and other promotional uses. For your book proposal, I recommended making a list called "endorsements," which is really a list of the people who *might* blurb your book. (There are also people who will recommend that you solicit actual blurbs for the proposal, long before publication, but I despise the extra unpaid work this practice levies on writers, and thus I do not recommend it.)

As you approach the point of publication and promotion, the blurb-request process enters the frame more concretely and your editor will cue you to collect some blurbs. (A quality editor or agent may also put their network into play by sending some blurb requests on your behalf.) At or before this time, you should refer to the list of names in your endorsements and distill it into a list of people you are actually comfortable emailing with a blurb request. You should also write an email template for this blurb request.

In my opinion, a blurb request should be complimentary, sincere, and utterly empathetic about the many demands on this author's time. In other words, it should specifically acknowledge *why* you are requesting this honor from this specific luminary, give them several months of lead time to read the book, and mention explicitly that you completely understand if they can't provide a blurb. It might read something like this:

```
Dear [author],


Our mutual friend bringing me to your reading at Green
Apple Books in San Francisco was an absolute highlight
of my spring 2023—as I mentioned in the signing line, I
was so happy you read the chapter about birdwatching
that changed my life forever.
    I'm excited to share the good news that my book
Debut, which also examines a life in birding, will be
published by Small but Mighty Press in fall 202X. Is
there any chance you'd consider writing a blurb for
this? If so, I'd be delighted to send you a digital or
physical copy—let me know which you'd prefer, and a
mailing address if you'd prefer hard copy.
    I realize that you probably receive 10,000 blurb
```

```
requests for every one you can fulfill, and please know

that I will admire you and your work forever whether or

not you're able to say yes to this one.

    Thank you so much for considering this!


[signature, with full contact info and medium

paragraph-long author bio below.]
```

A blurb request is a pitch, so it follows pitch praxis: Open with sincere compliments, connect your work and network to their work and network, get to the heart of your request fast, and respect your recipient's time by keeping the whole thing brief. Also, if you don't have an extensive relationship with the author you're asking to blurb, it's gracious to offer this kind of light reminder of when/where/how you met.

In her excellent book *Before and After the Book Deal: A Writer's Guide to Finishing, Publishing, Promoting, and Surviving Your First Book,* which I strongly recommend, author Courtney Maum outlines some very savvy insider tips about blurb requesting. If you don't have an MFA or a lot of writer contacts in your network, expect to get about three blurbs for every dozen requests you send. If you're a bit more established in a literary network, request your target number of blurbs plus three. If someone agrees to blurb your book, you're tacitly obliged to blurb theirs when the next opportunity arrives. Make sure to thank blurbers immediately with a handwritten note and/or small gift—don't wait until the book comes out. Then also send them a signed copy when the book does come out, with additional profuse thanks.

Maum also offers a bit of advice that I think represents commendable kindness and respect for fellow writers: If you are ever asked to blurb a book that, upon reading the book, you don't suspect you can earnestly praise, the correct response is always, *always* "I'm so sorry, I wasn't able to read this in time, but I wish you the best of luck with publication!" Blurb declines are the pinnacle of "If you can't say something nice, don't say anything at all."

Social Media: A Campaign of Bold Intrigue

Remember from the book proposal road map: Follower counts matter, yes, but so do civility, integrity, consistency, and originality. You should *not* start building your social media presence a month before your book appears in bookstores. Social media falls squarely in the camp of "marketing," which happens in an ongoing way for years.

It's nice to gain followers, but keeping them intrigued over the long run matters more. You are not tossing out a tweet once in a while. You are building a *campaign*.

Years in advance of your book's publication, beginning not later than the moment you sign a contract with a publisher, **commit to one or two social media channels that you will keep active.** Don't attempt to stay active on *all* of them unless you are prepared to dedicate a majority of your time to this—content creators who earn a living by posting a curated, edited daily video on YouTube, Instagram, TikTok, Facebook, X/Twitter, *and* Snapchat are definitely committing full-time hours (or more).

This part is important: **Choose channels that you enjoy and that play to your strengths.** Writers have long gathered on X/Twitter and Substack because we love text and fear cameras. Dancers and musicians flock to TikTok, Instagram, and YouTube for the exact inverse reason. Promotion will require spending more-than-usual time on social media, so you will have to jerry-rig your brain to *want* to do this. You will be most likely to succeed at this promotional binging in a venue where you are oriented, well connected, and comfortable.

Let me give you some concrete examples of what I mean. Aforementioned marketing genius Leigh Stein started creating content on TikTok two full years before *Self Care* was published. As she built her platform on TikTok, she took notice of the book-talkers who expressed a lot of enthusiasm for books by Sally Rooney, Ottessa Moshfegh, and Elif Batuman, who she thought had written reasonable comps for her book. Leigh hired a young college grad, trained her to support an outreach campaign, and personally contacted about one hundred of these BookTok accounts.

Leigh emphasizes that **while you can hire people to help execute your vision, the vision itself, and the contacts and personal initiative to enact it, have to come from** *you.* **"This** *cannot* **be outsourced,"** she says. While her assistant helped with research and legwork, the pitch emails came from Leigh herself, in her voice, with her unique insight and passion.

Here's another example of how a bold, intrigue-building publicity campaign can work. In advance of the thirty-day crowd-funding campaign that would ultimately persuade 767 backers to donate $81,160 for my film *Farah Goes Bang* in 2012, my team and I devised a content calendar that included the new release of *something, daily.* This was the Facebook era, so a typical week could include:

- **MONDAY:** Post a meme of Barack Obama wearing a shirt photoshopped to read *Farah Goes Bang.*

- **TUESDAY:** Post childhood photos of Meera and me emblazoned with a caption like *Don't you want to help these girls live their dreams???*
- **WEDNESDAY:** Release a new story on the blog we developed to accompany the campaign.
- **THURSDAY:** Publicize a new reward for twenty-five-dollar donors.
- **FRIDAY:** Post a behind-the-scenes video of Meera and me losing our minds in the preproduction office.
- **SATURDAY:** Post cat photos. So many photos of Meera's adorable cat. (RIP JFK, you served us nobly.)
- **SUNDAY:** Direct-message every single Facebook friend we have, asking them to cut and paste a message of support for our campaign as their status.

Every single one of these ridiculous marketing ploys included a link to our campaign. I sent so many private messages that Facebook thought I was a spambot and threatened to shut down my account.

This was hard, exhausting work that made me feel needy, exposed, and vulnerable. But the only thing worse than tearing my skin off live on Facebook was the possibility that we could fall short of our all-or-nothing goal, in which case I would surely regret any instinct to withhold. Our entire plan for making this movie was contingent upon succeeding in raising at least $75,000. So we went *hard* on every single one of those thirty days.

I have to share my single favorite comment I received on this campaign. A friend of a friend included this message with his twenty-five-dollar donation: "Dude, I know we weren't ever really that close, and I haven't talked to you in like forever, but holy shit your persistence is impressive. And your project is too. Therefore, you got me. I'm giving. YOU WIN . . . SHAMELESSNESS PAYS."

Here's what I take from this quote: Someone I knew in a peripheral way noticed my campaign, then heard so much about it that he was a little annoyed, then heard *so* much about it that his annoyance gave way to reluctant admiration. This provides a very handy analogue for how marketing, publicity, and advertising work. You have to worm your way into people's brains through *repetition.*

While relocating this quote in my inbox, I also happened across another comment on the campaign that floated back to me: "Jesus Christ, Laura is fucking spamming the shit out of me lately. What's with her?"

I include this less supportive comment to illustrate the unfortunate truth that any move into the public sphere will elicit pushback, and you should be as emotionally prepared as possible to withstand this inevitable pushback. You may be shocked to learn that a lot of people would really prefer that women, in particular, sit down, shut up, and keep our ambitions to ourselves! I knew, when I was sending so many messages that Facebook flagged my account, that some friends and acquaintances were probably flagging me too. So it goes. I wanted to make the movie of my dreams more than I wanted to people-please two thousand Facebook friends.

I also know that at the high-water mark of that "spamming," 86 friends reposted the status message I sent them. I know that 767 people were compelled to open their wallets. I know that multiple people donated multiple times. I know that our campaign placed in Kickstarter's top twenty most lucrative film fundraisers up to 2012. And I know that we raised enough money to *make the movie.*

There was another guy who scoffed at one of our producers, "You're trying to raise $75,000? Call me when *that* happens." And when we closed at $81,160, you bet your ass that we gave him a call. So I would also like to respond to this anonymous question: What is *with* her?

A finished feature film, one major festival premiere, one $25,000 prize at that premiere, eighteen other national and international film festivals, three Best Narrative Feature awards, the brilliant cast and crew who worked on that film, three books, the abiding love and support of the people who matter to me, and two middle fingers for anyone who dares to obstruct my dreams. *That's* what's with me.

Shamelessness pays.

Author-to-Author Partnerships

My second book, a tiny poetry collection called *Become a Name*, was released by an equally tiny publisher, Fathom Books, helmed by a longtime friend and MFA classmate. Fathom was planning to release my book at roughly the same time as *Swarm Queen's Crown*, a collection by my equally longtime friend and MFA classmate Stephanie Adams-Santos. So, naturally, Steph and I paired up to plan a release party: Seizing on her local connections, she set up the event at a Portland mead shop (of course Portland has a retailer that sells nothing but medieval honey wine), and together we invited everyone we knew in the area.

Let me tell you: I have never in my life seen that many people in one room for a *poetry* reading. I would estimate this was a crowd of roughly two hundred people, in a room so crowded some had to linger just outside the mead-shop windows. It helped mightily that Steph is a Portland native with a deep network: The audience included some of our MFA classmates and many of our word-nerd friends, yes, but also her entire family, the staff of pretty much every restaurant within a two-mile radius of her home, and her former students aged from their twenties to their eighties. Both of our small books sold well, largely as a result of that event.

The principle here is partnership: If you multiply your network by my network, we both get a bigger audience for our books. And this principle is hardly limited to two-author collaborations: During *Sister Mischief* promotion, another author friend, Molly Backes, generously invited me to guest-post on her blog *The Debutante Ball*, the header of which reads, "Seven Debut Authors. Seven Books. One Big Dance Toward Publication."

I've seen authors set up entire book tours where every event includes one or more collaborators, and this can dramatically widen the circle of buzz around a new book. You'll want to be careful and reciprocal in how you craft these partnerships: For some events, it may make sense to have two readers, while for others, it may make more sense to have a reader and an interviewer, so choose an author-partner with whom you can comfortably switch positions for various appearances. And the most effective author-to-author partnerships I've seen are multimedia: Two authors do some events together, and they *also* relentlessly plug each other's books on social media. Caretake somebody else's success as tenderly as you would your own and watch both of your victories multiply.

Charming Booksellers, Clubs, and Other Book Nerds of Influence

There is another important cadre of brilliant, underappreciated people who have the power to make or break your book:

independent booksellers. These are the bibliomaniacs who, if you treat them right, will hand-sell your book to untold numbers of people through readings, staff-pick shelves, personal recommendations, and other featured placements. There are books—*Women* by aforementioned heroine Chloe Caldwell is one of them—that have become bestsellers, cult classics, or re-releases, sometimes years after their original release, largely on the wings of bookseller admiration.

Long before you even have a book under contract, it's a great practice to know the independent bookstores in your area. Why not drop by, buy a great book, and make a casual inquiry about their upcoming event calendar and which employee coordinates their events? Why not make a recommendation to them about another book that's about to come out—one *not* by you—and offer to be that author's interviewer if she wants to do a store event? This ninja level of networking would not only greatly endear you to that author friend but also give you a backstage preview of this bookstore's event process. In short: Go to bookstores and make friends. Then, when your book comes out, you know just the right people to mail your advance reader copy (ARC) to with a personalized note.

ARCS

Advance reader or reading copies, also sometimes known as ARCs or galleys, are prepublication copies of a book that are sent out to VIPs to generate buzz ahead of a book's publication date. Commonly selected VIP recipients of these include book reviewers, social media influencers, authors who blurbed or otherwise endorsed your book, friends and family, and basically anybody who is at all likely to recommend purchasing your book to others. Generally, a publisher will generate both a hard copy and a digital copy, though as paper becomes more precious, digital copies are being pushed harder. ARCs almost always include a note with the disclaimer that the book's copy is not final and that reviewers should double-check any quotes for publication. In bookshelf practice, hard-copy ARCs are both a currency and a liability: They can Instagram-launch the inner circle of a particular book, but they can also pile up fast, and they can't be resold. If you're considering writing a review of a book, even for a small, personal blog or newsletter, emailing the publicity department of the book's publisher to say that will usually yield an ARC.

Everything I've just said about bookstores goes equally for libraries: They may not hand-sell books directly to your audience, but they sure can order one hundred copies of something they love, facilitate a book club or event around it, or make it your city's official One Read for the year. I know we are book children who revere libraries as silent, perfect spaces where we *don't* have to socialize, but when your book is about to be born, go to libraries to make friends too.

Book nerds of influence also gather in **book clubs,** which can meet either digitally or physically. You should *absolutely* write a list of discussion questions about your book for book clubs: You can provide this list for free on your website or even in the back-matter of the book itself if your publisher is amenable. You can also include some instructions on your website for where, when, and what kind of book clubs you'd be most excited to visit: I'm available for thirty-minute Zoom book club appearances from May through September, and I'll be thrilled to appear in yours if your book club can provide proof of purchase of ten copies of my book. You can also offer **insider perks** to book clubs, libraries, or other small groups: Maybe there's a cut chapter that you'd be willing to share with the right group, some publisher swag (tote bags, stickers, bookmarks) you can send their way, or an introduction to another author.

While we're talking about how to cover a *lot* of ground without leaving your house, **podcasts** are another huge opportunity to reach audiences. While you're assembling your publicity tool kit, make a list of podcasts, starting with the ones you listen to and love. Ask your friends for recommendations and add those too. Research the podcasts that have hosted other authors you love. Leigh Stein recommends an outstanding strategy for podcast outreach: Research the podcasts that your comp authors—in her case, Rooney, Moshfegh, and Batuman—appeared on, and pitch yourself to the podcasts on that list that seem most germane to you and your book.

As I write this in 2024, having survived a pandemic, I've seen nimble authors pivot entire IRL book tours to Zoom appearances with libraries, bookstores, book clubs, and podcasts. A manageable amount of advance work on your website can go miles to ingratiate you to these venues, so as you approach publication, update your website to include book club discussion questions, an ongoing list of digital and live appearances, your current availability, and how to book you.

Maximizing In-Person Events

I've already cautioned that in-person events tend not to sell as many copies as do innovative digital campaigns. That said, in-person events provide an irreplaceable opportunity to connect with live audiences of readers, and every author will do at least a few of these while promoting or touring. So let's talk through some best practices for live events.

At least eight weeks in advance of a bookstore event, make sure the bookstore has copies in stock or can get them in time for your reading. This may require that you give them a ballpark estimate of how many people you think will show up, so you (and your publicist, if applicable) should create event pages (on Evite, Facebook, etc.) with an RSVP function for any live event you plan. Be realistic in relaying these estimates. If you invited fifty people and fifteen RSVP'd, don't tell the bookstore you expect one hundred people—this will just leave them with overstock of your book and a sour taste in their mouth about you.

In advance, **practice reading aloud the chapter or chapters you'll read.** Time this practice so you know which chapter is fifteen minutes, which chapter is twenty, and which chapter is a tight seven. Make yourself fluent in reading several different chapters, because different excerpts will be appropriate to different venues: It was fun to read the chapter of *Sister Mischief* in which my protagonist's best friend teaches her to smoke weed to an audience of my friends, but my editor was not thrilled when I read it to a crowd of teenagers. Overall, select reading chapters that are as dramatic and punchy as possible. The funniest early chapter of your book is often an ideal choice for readings.

Do not ignore that your body plays a central role in these public events. An hour or two before the reading, eat a light meal with a noncarbonated, nonalcoholic beverage. (It is impossible to treat your digestive system *too* well during a barrage of live events.) Budget your energy while touring; don't overbook multiple events in the same area unless they have demonstrably different audiences, be careful of overpromising drinks or dinner to friends around readings, and prioritize sleep and down time. Develop an event wardrobe in which you feel comfortable and cute. For me, this means nothing too restrictive, nothing that shows sweat stains, more makeup (for cameras) and less jewelry (for microphones) than I'd wear to teach, polished nails, and comfortable socks and shoes. My antimaterialistic feminism and midwestern frugality collude here to emphasize that none of this has to be expensive or time-consuming. I'm a big fan of the press-on acrylic nails you can get from Walgreens for eight dollars and apply in thirty seconds.

Keep your reading brief and entertaining: You don't want to exhaust your audience, you want to leave them wanting more so badly that they *have* to buy your book. I do not think that a bookstore event should devote more than twenty minutes to reading from the book. Open by offering a moment of orientation in the book's whole story, but don't overintroduce: If the chapter requires fifteen minutes of paraphrased backstory in order to make sense, you've picked the wrong chapter to read aloud. Read more slowly than feels natural, impart some dramatic pauses, and make a near-obscene level of eye contact with your audience. Parry with them. Charm them.

Allow me to step onto a soapbox for a moment here. Many writers are *abysmal* readers. This is a pet peeve of mine, so much so that I wonder about its connection to these events' sales records. To be a writer is a deeply private thing. But to be a reader, even for an audience of three at a tiny bookstore, is to be a *performer,* and that is definitionally public. I have a calculated idea of what I like to wear to a public event because I know from my experience in the performing arts how alchemically helpful the right wardrobe can be in constructing a confident persona. I know I need to speak with unnatural slowness because I know I usually speak with unnatural speed. In sum, I have gotten to know my performer self well enough to give her the tools she needs, and as bizarre as it can feel to practice all this for your bedroom mirror, I forcefully recommend you do so. In readings as in pitches, auditions, and introductions, never, ever apologize—in words, or with your embarrassed tone, messy hair in your face, downturned eyes, or mumbled enunciation. Square your shoulders, smile, and project from the diaphragm. **If you want to sell creative work, learn to command a room's attention.**

After the selected reading, you or your interlocutor will gracefully cue the audience that you're open to questions. And boy howdy, if you thought I had loud opinions about events, buckle up for my thoughts on Q&As.

Audience Q&As are sites of rich illumination and also emotional terrorism for writers. These are the democratic spaces where your friend's dad is just as entitled to comment that your book had too much sex as is a local English professor who wishes to praise your command of Derrida. As you bodysurf this volatile space, I want you to hold fast the truth that **you control this conversation.** You are 100 percent in charge of what you will and will not discuss. **You never, ever have to answer the exact question that was asked;** this isn't *60 Minutes.* It is completely acceptable to answer the blowhard comment about how there's too much sex with a sentence such as "Thank you so much for that invitation to reflect on my craft choices. I'd say my biggest literary influences for that passage were Kathy Acker and Patricia Highsmith. Next question?"

I recommend that you commit some detailed, in-advance thought to two categories: the topic areas you are most excited to

discuss, and the topic areas you absolutely will not discuss. Speaking broadly, if you get a question that falls into the no-discussion zone, your task is just to edge it into your preferred talking points, as I just illustrated.

For me personally, there are three audience questions that I have heard many times before and that I absolutely, categorically will not answer. They are:

- How do your parents feel about your book?
- How does your husband feel about your book?
- How do your children feel about your book?

Honestly, even transcribing those questions makes my blood boil, because they are *so frequently* lobbed at women writers who write about issues our culture deems "sensitive." And make no mistake: Whether their asker is conscious of this intent or not, these questions are cattle prods of shame aimed at keeping women in a deferential place.

If I were to answer that question at face value, I would say that my father, mother, ex-husband, and two children have published, between all five of them, a grand total of zero books, and the content of the one I've published is what we're here to discuss. On a patient day, I might charmingly quip that I'm *much* more interested in *your* thoughts on this book than in my family's. I might also note that I've learned from the many twelve-steppers I love that other people's opinions about me or my work are simply none of my business. From there, I would almost certainly transition into an impassioned lecture about how the impact of these questions is diminishing ambitious women, and by the time I reached that lecture's end, I would surely be breathless with fury and loath to continue the group interview.

You see: I've gotten to know my performer self well, and I know what she can and cannot abide.

I don't want to be contentious with an audience; I'm not appearing before them to prove I can win an argument. So I've discerned that it takes a lot less energy to say, "That's none of my business," or "Thank you so much for that invitation to reflect on my craft choices," than it does to meta-interrogate the unfairness of the question. You are entitled to determine what you will and will not discuss, and to uphold that boundary.

Audiences can be unpredictable in book-signing lines just as they are in Q&As, so for a busy event it can be helpful to recruit a friend or bookstore employee to keep the signing line moving. Establish a quick, benign tradecraft phrase ("My goodness!") with the line-mover that means "I'm done with this person, please move them along."

A few final tips and tricks for live events:

- The easiest way to avoid epidemics of "This is more of a comment than a question" gasbaggery is to facilitate the Q&A by asking attendees to write down their questions on a notecard. Filter those notecards yourself or recruit a trusted emcee.
- In advance of publication and events, print business cards with your book cover, email, and website link. Bring those everywhere you go. Slip them into signed books as bookmarks.
- Bring five Sharpies everywhere you go too.
- If the event is not at a bookstore, tag a friend to help staff the sales table—this is a lot to handle yourself while you're also signing books and chatting.
- Create a sign-up mechanism for your newsletter at the

event itself—a QR code, a visible link, or an analog pen-and-paper sign-in sheet.

One Book Is Only One Chapter of a Career

Late in our conversation, Leigh made an offhand comment that landed hard with me.

"Newcomers are obsessed with selling as soon as possible," she said. "Veterans know this is a long career. It's not just about one book. Do you want to publish a memoir, or do you want to be a professional writer?"

This zoomed-out, big-picture perspective, I've found, can be so, so useful in tempering the kind of urgent, keyed-up anxiety that accompanies Big Moments, like a debut release. One book is *one book*. It might be a Pulitzer-winning bestseller, or it might be a quiet, proud gathering of your closest friends in your bestie's backyard. Print is permanent, so it's wise to take your time committing your words to paper. Print is cheap, so the words you put to paper might be tomorrow's kindling. Like the story of the little boy and the Zen master, we'll see.

Your book may feel like your whole heart, but it's not your whole life. Do your best to promote it in a creative, wholehearted way, then go home to the people you love and eat some dinner.

CHAPTER 8

Being Your Own Boss

Negotiating, Getting Paid, and Staying Organized

Under the oft-mentioned category of "things no one taught me in my MFA," "how to obtain actual money" might just be the #1 entry. While I obviously think it's important to examine how to introduce yourself with confidence and target a strategic pitch, I would be remiss if I didn't spend some time talking about **cold hard cash:** How do we get it, how do we make more of it, how do we keep track of it?

I can't give you all the answers, but I can be honest with you about my own experience: I've considered myself a professional writer for about twenty years, and the writing I want to do most has never made up more than a minority of my income. I have had day jobs, night jobs, side jobs, and various forms of support from my partner and family. Very few writers and artists—like less than 1 percent of writers and artists—ever make their living exclusively from the writing they want to do most. I say all this to highlight that **"success" in an artistic field is not equivalent to making your entire living in that field.** In addition, writers who do nothing but sit alone in a dark room might find themselves with very little to write about.

Writers unequivocally deserve to be paid for their time and work. But it's a frustrating reality of writing life that to obtain access to the publications that pay, you'll probably have to write for some publications that don't. I finished my MFA when I was twenty-four, worked a full-time journalism/communications job for two years after that, then went full-time freelance when I was twenty-six and had signed my first book deal. I did not feel equipped to declare, "I'm not writing anything for free anymore" until after I had my first baby, when I was thirty.

Not writing for free anymore was one of the best decisions I've ever made, but unfortunately it was a decision I had to spend years earning the professional stature to make. Also, when I say I don't write for free anymore, I really mean that I don't publish short-form pieces for free anymore—of course any long-form book or screenplay I write is written for free unless and until someone decides to buy it from me. Being a writer, even a "successful" writer, always entails some measure of unpaid work, so I think it's essential for writers to have multiple income streams, including day jobs and side hustles.

Here are some venues where I have sometimes chosen to work for no money, especially early in my career:

- In my personal blog or newsletter.
- In exchange for goods or services—I've written for free food/drinks, nice trips, and bartered favors, such as writing a blog post for an illustrator friend with the understanding that he'd throw me an illustration for another piece.
- For a publication that seemed like the work of good

people even though it didn't pay, after I'd unsuccessfully pitched a few that did. Or when I was pitching a piece that I just wanted to have out there. An example: I once published a personal essay called "Emergency Pot Cookie" on *Vela* even though I wasn't paid because the editors seemed great and I'd already gotten passes from *NYMag* and *BuzzFeed* for the essay's lack of timely urgency. I knew it wasn't a particularly newshooky piece, and I just wanted to get it out there, so *Vela* seemed like my best option. The piece ended up getting mentioned in *The New York Times*.

- When I was trying to assemble a bouquet of three or four solid bylines, early in my career, so I could build my profile for paying publications. I know this sucks, and I wish it were otherwise, but dues paying is real. Cheryl Strayed wrote *Dear Sugar* for free.

- On a project that wouldn't leave me alone, and that I cared about too much to leave undone even if no one ever paid me a single red cent for it. Again: Cheryl Strayed wrote *Dear Sugar* for free.

You'll notice that this list of places for which I have been willing to work for no money is distinctly limited. Overall, I cannot and do not want to work for free, so let's talk about **negotiation**. My friend and collaborator Meera claims I am great at negotiation because my strict Catholic parents gave me so much early experience in negotiating later curfews. Meera is rarely wrong.

Here's where you're standing in this scenario: You've sent your incredibly well-researched pitch to a deftly selected editor, and that editor has written you back saying they'd like to publish your piece! Hooray! And also: WTF do you do now? Because so little is said about negotiation in any other resource for writers that I've ever sought, and also because of my unresolved Catholic trauma, I have a *lot* to say on this subject.

Negotiation Best Practices for Writers*

Unless the publication specifies a standardized, nonnegotiable rate, **you absolutely do not have to accept an opening offer.** You may not always succeed in negotiating your rate upward, but I contend that it's always worthwhile to *try.* If the editor offers $50 for a two-thousand-word reported piece, you are perfectly entitled to write back and say something like "For something of this length/depth, $250 would be closer to what I'd imagined," or even "I really can't take less than $400 for something like this." You may or may not get the exact rate you name, but I've found that many reputable editors can be negotiated up.

I also think there's an unwritten rule at play here: **Inexperienced writers are less likely to negotiate, and** *experienced editors know this.* Therefore, you stand a greater chance of being taken seriously as a professional simply by demonstrating that you're willing and able to negotiate for yourself. Negotiation is a form of skilled self-advocacy, and you'll get better at it the more you do it—so do it.

Broadly speaking, you're in the stronger negotiating position if you **let the other party open with a first offer**—this editor knows how much they can afford to offer and you don't, so you don't want to undercut yourself by quoting $200 in case they were going to offer $400 before you opened your big mouth. Let your editor

---

*   Apply these best practices *after* an editor has expressed interest in publishing one of your pieces.

name the first figure. Don't be afraid to answer questions with questions: If an editor says, "What's your rate?," you can always respond with "What do you typically pay for pieces like this?" It can feel uncomfortable to hold the line like this, but it can also yield results.

As you already know, 99.9 percent of the communication you'll ever have with editors will take place by email. So to negotiate by email, I've named my operative principle here the "**triangulated email**." Picture an upside-down pyramid or Dwayne Johnson's silhouette: Most of the bulk is at the top, then it narrows. You want the shape of your email to get the editor as invested as possible in how beneficial you and your work will be to them and their publication, and *then* you want that investment to result in a maximized rate.

The opening paragraph of your triangulated email leads with all the great work you're going to do in this piece for this editor: "Hi [editor], I was so excited to get this response. I'm really intrigued by your feedback on X and could imagine incorporating it in YZ specific and compelling ways. Yes, I think the timeline you propose is completely reasonable—I can get a draft to you by [deadline the editor suggested], if not sooner."

Then, after you've whipped the editor into thrills over how easy and fun it will be to collaborate with you, you conclude with a brief, piercing appraisal of your work's value. "In order to prioritize this over other work, I'll need $X." Or "To give this story the research and reporting it deserves, I really can't take less than $X." Or "Actually, I was recently paid [$200 more than the editor offered] for a story of similar length and depth. Could you meet me at [increased rate]?"

When naming rates, be very clear, direct, and brief. Equivocations and niceties in this section of the email will only weaken your position. Never name more than one figure—"Um, I was really hoping for \$300–\$400 for this, but if \$150 is the best you can do, I understand"—because decision-makers will latch onto the lowest figure. Don't ramble beyond your price quote; name your figure and *get out*.

In other words, your triangulated email to an editor who's expressed interest in your piece is one line about how excited you'd be to work with them, one paragraph intelligently responding to their specific concerns and making yourself seem enthusiastic and indispensable, and then one sentence on price negotiation at the end. Signature. Send.

Here's how this might read:

```
Dear [editor],

This email absolutely made my day. Thank you so much
for this swift and positive response. I can't wait to
hit the ground running with this story.

    I think you make a strong point about how this story
needs more than two interviews to present a balanced
view; in addition to the sources I suggested in my
initial pitch, I could imagine interviewing a contact I
have at Reuters (an old friend who owes me about ten
favors) and asking them to refer me to three to five
other people. And yes, I think the timeline you propose
is completely reasonable; I can get a draft to you by
the end of the month, if not sooner. I'll also plan to
share docs of my source interviews between now and then
```

```
so you stay apprised of where I'm headed with this. I'm
already so appreciative of your feedback!

    To prioritize this writing and reporting over other
work, I don't think I can take less than $500. Could
you meet me there?


All best, and many thanks again,
L.
```

Talking About Money

Do *not* assume that the editor will bring up the subject of payment, or that if they don't bring it up, there's no compensation available. As I mentioned in our chapter 5 discussion of short-form pitches, **compensation should *always* be discussed after acceptance of the pitch and before publication of the story. This holds true even if you have to be the person to raise the subject.** I mean, if you never bring it up, they never have to pay you, right? If the prospect of asking for money makes you uncomfortable, you're in great company: Very few writers choose this profession on the basis of a passion for economics.

Once compensation is discussed, a contract should shortly follow; even small publications usually have some kind of simple contract. (A very tiny, informal, or niche publication may not, in which case documentation of the rate and story agreement by email usually suffices.) A good editor who's on top of that day's to-do list should send the contract along as soon as the story's length and rate are agreed upon, but don't be afraid to prompt it yourself. As with all things, do not ever, ever, *ever* sign something you don't fully understand. If you're embarrassed to keep lobbing questions at your potential editor, enlist friends, teachers, or mentors. Friends who went to law school can be particularly helpful here, should you have any.

The most salient detail to look for in a contract is when the publication or corporation commits to paying you. Most publications' contracts say that they'll pay in the vicinity of thirty days. Read the fine print on this—is it thirty business days ("Net 30") or thirty calendar days ("T 30")?—and don't be afraid to ask questions before you sign.

Also, scan all contracts for language that details *when* you can submit your invoice and start the thirty-day clock. Is this upon publication? Is it when your editor signs off on her edits? Absent any specific language like this in the contract, submit your invoice as soon as you receive any indication that editing and writing work on your piece are complete.

I also recommend you look out for the following:

- **KILL FEES.** 25 percent is standard if a kill fee is offered.
- **RIGHTS SHARES.** Does the publication own all exclusive rights to this piece in perpetuity? Do reprint rights revert back to the author after six months? Does the publication own the TV, film, or audio rights?
- **PERMISSIONS AND LICENSES.** Most editorial contracts include a clause that amounts to "You, the author, are responsible for your work's accuracy, and for obtaining permission to use all the material within it, and you agree that we, the publication, cannot be sued if you get any of this wrong." This has become more common as publications have shed internal fact-checkers (deep sigh

for democracy). If you need the publication to absorb any costs of fact-checking or permissions, do your best to negotiate for that on the front end.

- **MODE OF PAYMENT.** It's wise to ask if direct deposit is an option for payment or to accept it if it's offered—this can get you paid seven to ten days faster than waiting for a check to arrive in the mail and then clear your bank account, and you're also guaranteed not to lose it in the mail or forget to deposit it.

After you've read any contract carefully, especially when it comes to payment language, save all contracts in hard copy or a designated file folder on your hard drive. Many publications use digital-signing services that will save a copy of your signed contract for only a few months.

Let me play out a worst-case scenario of the potential cost of avoiding talking about money or contracts. You pitch a dream editor of a well-known publication on a juicy story you've been holding in the chamber for a long time. An hour later, the editor jumps on the story and launches into edits, which are fantastic and make your story even better than you'd imagined. Things are moving fast and you feel like it'd be rude to bring up money—and honestly, getting this story out there was never about the money for you anyway. You assume the editor is a professional, so they'll probably bring it up eventually, and you just continue with the editing process. You don't want to seem difficult, after all.

Suddenly, your story is published. It goes viral. An executive at Hulu emails you asking to read the terms of your contract for your story because they're interested in optioning it for a series adaptation. You respond with the truth: You have no contract. Hulu promptly loses your email and proceeds directly to the publication that ran your story, which owns all exclusive rights to it. Hulu and the publication go on to make millions of dollars on your story, which makes the screenwriter of the adaptation, conspicuously not you, a household name. In the series, you're credited as the author of the original story as a legal courtesy, but you are never paid a cent for a production that made other people rich and famous.

Do you see where I'm going with the importance of not avoiding the topic of compensation? Don't avoid it, don't assume that the editor will bring it up, and don't assume that the first offer an editor makes is the most they're able to offer.

I will volunteer that I talk about money more eagerly and often than most artists, maybe than most people. It's understandable to wonder why any of us should bother with the boring business of bean-counting when we have limited, valuable time to devote to our art itself. I *vastly* prefer nurturing my creative process to sending invoices or filing taxes. However, I staunchly reject the popular conception of authors as flaky, flighty alcoholics who can't be bothered with financial realities.

I make it a point to talk about money because my upbringing and education in largely white-dominated environments offered me a certain measure of financial literacy, and thus **I consider the candid sharing of financial literacy tools to be an act of class and race rebellion**. It is only the people born too rich to ever worry about food insecurity who have the privilege of considering financial discussions unseemly. I am proud to have published a book of poetry, and I am also proud to be able to contribute $200 a month to my stock portfolio, but only one of these is likely to aid in my retirement or to cover the surprise ER bill if my son ever decides to shove a pom-pom up his nose again. I believe I have developed a reputation as an operator who never accepts a first offer, and I'm proud of that too. I do not believe in equating one's personal worth as a human being with capitalistic productivity or income. But no one will ever insist upon my worth, in any sense, except me, so it behooves me to know how to make that insistence in as many senses as possible.

I can name far too many poets fielding six-figure student loan tabs, too many novelists shocked to owe 30 percent of their book advance to the government on April 15, and too many essayists regretful about selling the most personal details of their trauma for $150 to pretend that economic savvy has no bearing on artistic viability. As Sugar herself told us: "You don't have to maintain an impeccable credit score," but you do "have to pay your own electric bill." We are professionals, and a professional handles her business.

So now that we've internalized the ethical reasons for speaking freely about money, how do we actually *get more*? Previous payment information—either what you've been paid at other publications for a similar assignment or what you know other people have been paid at this publication—is your best friend and biggest point of leverage in negotiation. Consult whopayswriters.com for payment information on any publication you're considering, ask your friends what they made from specific publications, and ask for rates commensurate with what you've made for similar pieces elsewhere in the past. Another helpful rubric is the editorial rates listed by the Editorial Freelancers Association, which outline reasonable rates by page, word, and hour.

Also, be sure to incorporate any relevant costs entailed by your story into your rate. If you can't reasonably execute your story without incurring some sort of travel, equipment, or research expenses, those costs should absolutely be shouldered by the publication. Clarify whether you'll accept a flat rate—$1,000 for writing a three-thousand-word reported story, inclusive of a plane ticket and an interview transcription assistant—or an assignment rate plus expenses—$800 for the story, plus travel and research expenses up to $250 to be reimbursed with receipts upon invoicing.

Finally, use timing and news-cycle currency to your advantage in negotiating, especially if an editor wants a very quick turnaround. I've gotten double my typical rate for pieces on hot-button issues that needed to be turned around in less than forty-eight hours.

Sometimes you will find yourself in a negotiating position without any of these data points or assets. In those cases, don't be afraid to just double the proposed rate: $400 isn't really all that much more than $200. Fortune favors the bold.

As you considered them in pitching, consider the size and stature of the publication at hand when negotiating rates too. Be realistic in both directions: Small publications won't have a lot to pay, and big publications are highly skilled in obtaining your work for as little as possible. Some small publications categorically do not pay contributors, or pay a standardized, nonnegotiable rate; if this is the case, they almost always say so very clearly on their submission pages.

Big-name publications, however, especially those owned by big corporations, have real money, and freelance labor comes cheap. Remember, when you freelance for them, they're not paying for your ongoing salary, healthcare, or any other perks—food, office space, technology, bonuses—available to regular employees. I've at times been so dazzled to get a yes from a big publication that I've blown right past the part where I should have negotiated for more money. Again, just as experienced editors know that in-experienced writers don't negotiate, they also know that prestige is a currency that can swindle the inexperienced into accepting less cash. Don't let big companies convince you they're too poor to pay you decently, and by the same token, don't expect big payouts from scrappy journals.

There is a clear frontrunner in the category of questions I am most often asked about negotiation: *If I negotiate, will the editor get so annoyed that they rescind their offer?*

First, I want to flag that this is an incredibly common concern. I would cite this as a frequent iteration of the "Will people be mad at me" question I referenced in chapter 1, and also as probably the second-most common question of all my time teaching pitching, following only "Should I write the story or the pitch first?"

It's been my experience that reputable editors are not at all alienated by thoughtful negotiation and that many of them are very much in favor of increasing writers' compensation. I've certainly had editors decline my proposed rate and have still chosen to work with some of them, but I've never had an editor just roll up an offer and walk away because I asked for more money. In most cases, the worst that can happen is the editor will just stick to their original figure. Anybody who *would* rescind an offer because an author had the audacity to argue for her worth is simply not somebody you want to work with.

Try to think of it this way: By the time you've gotten a decision-maker interested enough to convey that interest to you by discussing rates, you have the power position, even if it may feel otherwise. To make you an offer, they've probably had to get approval from their higher-ups, which means they've already expressed their enthusiasm for your idea and put their credibility on the line. If it doesn't work out with you, they may have to find someone else to write on this topic, which means more work for them. Remember how I said editors need writers more than writers need editors?

I've had only one actual experience with a decision-maker rescinding an offer due to negotiation in my entire career. While preparing our film for distribution, Meera and I met with several distribution agents. One of them offered us representation and sent over a prospective term sheet; I responded with several rounds of detailed questions on the term sheet, because I never sign anything I don't fully understand. Abruptly, the agent sent back an email saying, in effect, "I'm retracting this offer because you seem like too much trouble; have a nice life." This was disappointing in the moment, of course, but not very long afterward, we found a different agent who was delighted to answer all my questions. The moral of the story here, to me, is that negotiation is a filtration mechanism: Ultimately, I don't want to collaborate with anyone who thinks that clarifying the nature of an agreement is too much trouble.

All of this said, there does exist such a thing as *too* much negotiation. I almost never go more than one round of negotiation with the same gatekeeper. If I pitch an evergreen story, the editor opens with $200, I counter with $400, and they counter-counter with $300, then I can see that they've made a good-faith effort to increase my rate, and I'm probably going to take the $300. The only reason I *wouldn't* accept that $300 is if I had good reason to suspect I could make more elsewhere. In that scenario, I'd move my negotiation efforts to a second editor, rather than continuing to try to ratchet the first editor upward.

Never forget the bedrock rule of negotiation: **She who is willing to walk away holds all the power.** Don't be afraid to walk away if an editor won't come within a reasonable distance of a justifiable rate. If I ask for $500 and an editor says the best they can do is $400, I'll usually take it. But if they say they can offer $75 and great exposure and maybe more money when they raise a Series C next year, I'm going to thank them for their consideration and decline. Keep emotion out of your negotiation language as much as possible. This is a business transaction; it's not personal. Maintain relentless positivity and courtesy—don't ever respond with snark, anger, offense, or passive-aggression, even if you're declining an offer. You'd be shocked at how often a polite decline is met with a more desirable offer.

In rare cases, you may receive multiple offers on the same story. This is a great scenario: bidding war, baby! This doesn't happen often, but you should absolutely leverage multiple offers against each other if you receive more than one. "Hey there [Editor 1], I'm so excited you like the piece, but I wanted to let you know that [Publication 2] has offered me a higher rate for it. To be candid, I've been dying to work with you—is there any way you could offer [$100 more than Editor 1 offered]?"

Check Chasing 101, aka Getting Paid

I wish so much that the issue of collecting money you're contractually and legally owed didn't merit its own section, but in my experience it does. Chasing down checks can be the single most frustrating part of being a freelancer, and every freelancer I know has had at least one panicky situation of the rent coming due while four unpaid invoices ripple in the wind. Sigh.

Remember: **Check chasing starts with the contract you sign.** Your first order of check-chasing business is to refer to the contract you signed (and understood and saved to your hard drive) to see if this publication will pay you in thirty days, in thirty business days, or on another timeline. Set a calendar reminder to follow up one day after the payment deadline: I hope this won't be necessary, but experience has showed me it often is.

Maintain a current W9 and standard invoice on file for yourself, and submit as soon as you and your editor close out edits on your piece or it goes live, depending on the publication's contract language. Unless otherwise specified, a W9 and invoice should be enough to pay you, and *do not* feel like you have to wait for an editor to ask for them before sending them along—hesitating on the issue only delays when your thirty-day pay cycle begins.

My standard editorial invoice looks like this:

EDITORIAL INVOICE

Submit Date: 9/30/2022

Invoice #: 093022LG

Organization:

Name: Laura Goode

Mailing Address:

Project Name	Amount	Description
Organization, Department	$X	Feature writing: on X, Y, and Z

Total Amount Due: $X

Also, remember that your BFF in check chasing is your handy submissions tracking document, which looks something like this:

Essay/Pitch	Publication	Editor	Date	Sim Subs?	Results	Payment Due	Invoiced	Payment Rec'd?
My Teen Mom Feeling	ELLE	Chloe Schama	12/29/2015	No	YES	$300	1/12/2016	3/14/2016
Interview with James Kaelan	Bright Ideas	Nicole Malek	1/1/2016	No	YES	$200	1/15/2016	3/28/2016

Use this document to record how much you're owed and the date you submitted your invoice in your submissions tracker; then, when you eventually get paid, *also* record the date you received payment. I promise you'll thank yourself later when you have to hunt down a late check, collect pay stubs and 1099s for taxes, compare which publications pay the most or fastest for future work, or share any of this information with others—which, as you're now thoroughly convinced, is very much in your best interests to do. A publication that pays a lot has obvious value; a publication that pays promptly has subtler but equally relevant value.

For neurotic bonus points, set a calendar reminder for the day your payment is due from a specific publication. At least refer regularly back to your submission tracker to see when you submitted your invoice. That way, when day 31 rolls around and you still haven't been paid—and it will—you can follow up right away.

Though I fervently wish this were not the case, my experience instructs me to instruct you on how to write a follow-up email indicating that you are past due on payment. My opinions on this subject have intensified with experience. I used to write follow-up emails that went something like this:

```
Hi [editor]!

Hope you're well. I don't mean to be a pest, but I was
just wondering about the $400 payment for the story
that I published with you last month. I haven't yet
received it. Could you give me an update on when I can
expect to receive it?
     Also, the piece you just published on homicidal pet
groomers was hilarious. :)

Many thanks, and all best,
L.
```

The example I provided above is how a people-pleaser pleads for money she's due. Here is a more assertive way to convey the same information:

```
Hello.

The contract I signed with your publication on DATE
indicated that I would be paid for my work within
thirty days of submitting my invoice and W9. Thirty
days have now passed since I submitted all
documentation on DATE. Please alert the appropriate
colleagues that this deadline has passed so this matter
can be resolved. Please confirm receipt of this email
so I know this is being handled. I appreciate your
prompt attention to this matter and look forward to its
efficient resolution.
```

This is a boss move. I *aspire* to this level of bad bitch.

If you take nothing else from my ranting about money, please remember this advice: **Do not *ever* feel like you are being rude, pushy, or a pest for following up on money you are contractually/legally owed.** Wait until the thirty-day window has passed, but on day 31, send a brief, polite email.

Don't be afraid to follow up more than once—if the editor responds to your first follow-up by saying you should expect a check by the end of next week, set a reminder to follow up next Friday if you haven't received the check by then. Be cordial but be persistent—if an editor is tasked with responding to your continued emails, they're likelier to make sure you get paid.

If you have to follow up multiple times, ask the editor if they can refer you to a contact in their accounting department. "Hey Editor, I hate to keep harassing you for this check—would it be possible for you to put me in touch with your accounting department directly so I can make sure they have everything they need?"

Time for one of Laura's bitter anecdotes from the past! I once waited *sixteen weeks* for a relatively large check from a very well-known publication, where the editor was a dear and longtime friend, because I kept harassing my friend about the check and it turned out she had straight-up forgotten to submit my invoice to accounting. Sometimes even a great editor is less useful to getting you paid than an accounting contact who can confirm whether they have your paperwork or not.

Negotiation Case Studies

I'm always on the hunt for resources for my "Pitching and Publishing in Popular Media" course, and for *years* I've hunted for any sort of negotiation case studies for writers. All I've ever found is

Harvard Business Review articles angled toward consultants and CFOs, so I built some writer-specific case studies myself.

As you read the following hypotheticals, start your negotiation by trying to identify the **relevant data points**. In other words, what pieces of information might affect price negotiation? Then use those data points to determine what your options are and what the best option is.

Case Study #1

You're pitching a two-thousand-word personal essay to *Murder Horse,* a small but prestigious online publication. The essay is evergreen and without a timely news hook. The publication offers you $150. You counter with $300, but the editor says $150 is their flat rate and they don't negotiate with anyone. Other friends who've written for *Murder Horse* confirm this, and you've never been paid for a story before.

What are your options here?

Analysis

The most relevant data point here is the publication's flat rate. Especially because this flat rate seems consistent with the publication's "small but prestigious" profile, and also because it has been verified by others, you clearly do not have leverage to negotiate a price upward with *Murder Horse.*

Also relevant is that you, the author, do not have a mechanism for negotiating the price upward on the basis of the story itself: It's long, it's a personal essay, it's more evergreen than timely, and you don't have a prior rate to quote.

From all this, I would assess that the most beneficial route for a first-time author here would be to accept the flat rate, publish a prestigious *Murder Horse* story, and use that success to support future pitches elsewhere. A second option would be to send a polite decline to *Murder Horse* and try to pitch the story elsewhere for more money, but this seems riskier to me.

Case Study #2

A friend-of-a-friend editor at the buzzy political outlet *Your Mom Should Run* emails you at 11 a.m. on a Tuesday. She asks if you have any interest in writing a story on a topic you've written about before that's just popped back into the news. The topic is very timely, related to an election news cycle, and the editor asks you to turn around eight hundred words by the end of business *today*. She offers $350. Your day is already busy with other paid work, but you're intrigued by the editor/publication.

How do you respond?

Analysis

This is a case where you have some leverage! You have multiple elements working in your favor here: The topic is timely, you have established credibility on the topic, and the editor wants this story *fast*. From this, we can deduce that if you decline, the editor is likely to have to go back to the drawing board to find someone else to write on this topic, which will only put them farther behind in the news cycle.

Also, while this case study doesn't specify your previous rates, it does indicate that you're fielding other work, so you genuinely do need this gig to be worth your while in order to sideline some of that work.

All in all, this is an opportunity to negotiate *hard*. I would recommend responding to the effect that you can meet the tight turnaround for double your rate, in this case $700. Then I would clear your schedule for the day, do a fantastic job delivering the story with speed and quality, and use $700 as your starting rate for all future stories with this editor.

Case Study #3

You're pitching a four-thousand-word feature about a rising-star celebrity. You have unique access to this celebrity through an unusual personal connection—you happened to go to camp together as kids and have stayed in loose touch—and they're involved in a high-profile project set to debut in three months. You don't want to take less than $1,000 for this story; you know your connection is valuable, plus you recently got burned when you accepted $400 for a similarly interview-heavy story and it ate up a lot of time. The first outlet you pitch, Sam at *Prost!*, seems the most promising in terms of fit and audience, but doesn't get back to you right away. After a week, you pitch a second target, Ro at *Dog Leg Mag,* a solid but slightly less exciting publication. Ro responds enthusiastically within a day and offers $500.

How do you proceed?

Analysis

This is another case where you have some leverage: You have enough experience to be able to assess the viability of past rates, and you have a valuable, unusual connection to a high-wattage subject. And the enthusiastic response from *Dog Leg Mag* confirms the value of your story.

You have a few options here. First, you could just accept *Dog Leg*'s $500 offer. Or you could simply ask for more money from *Dog Leg:* "Actually, given the value of this connection, I'll need at least $1,000 for this." This could work, but it doesn't apply any specific pressure to that editor.

Another option would be to go back to Sam at *Prost!* "Hi there, I've received another offer on this piece, but I'm still really curious to hear your thoughts. Could you let me know by the end of the day whether you're still considering this piece?" If *Prost!* responds with an offer greater than $500, you can accept it or try to negotiate upward. If *Prost!* responds with an offer less than $500, you can accept *Dog Leg*'s offer, or use *Dog Leg*'s proposed rate to negotiate *Prost!* upward. If *Prost!* doesn't respond by your stated deadline, then you know *Dog Leg* is your best option.

ASSIGNMENT

- Catch up on anything you haven't finished so far: readings, your bio, website, newsletter, shout-outs, pitch, or query.
- Research payment information from whopayswriters.com and/or your contacts for a few publications that interest you.

CHAPTER 9

Break Glass in
Case of Emergency

The Fire Extinguishers of Emotional
Regulation That Every Writer Needs

How shall I leave you? I've poured twenty years of hard-earned creative professional principles into this book, and soon you will close its back cover having inherited pretty much everything I've ever learned about making a living as a writer.

Because I still feel quite emphatically that success as a professional creative rests as much on emotional and psychological regulation as it does on entrepreneurial savvy, I've preserved a few savory life-of-a-writer stories just for this moment, the book's valedictory breath. These stories represent the ways I've encountered some of the nonpoverty forces that can sink a writer, and my strategies for vanquishing them. This chapter provides the fire extinguishers you pull out when the vehicle of your ego, work ethic, or stamina hits a tree and bursts into flames—and if you're doing your job with courage and dedication, it surely will. Read on to write on.

Jealousy and Envy

These are invisible snakes around the ankles of every writer: writhing, slippery, omnipresent, and liable to trip us if we don't stomp them first. Let me be candid. I hold two degrees from a starfucker university, where my classmates included Greta Gerwig, Vampire Weekend, Jenny Slate, Julia Stiles, and Kate McKinnon. One of my closest friends from college is currently directing a Netflix series. I saw another old college friend in a touring Broadway production recently, and what was the first thing we talked about after embracing? How hard it can be to keep the faith in our own feeble dreams in the face of our peers' screaming global success. A working Broadway actor and the author of three books had this conversation: We ain't shit compared to those superstars.

I love brilliant, talented, creative, complicated people, and what this means is that I've had to do a lot of internal, ongoing work on my own capacity to be genuinely happy for other people's success. This work has precipitated some *very* uncomfortable examinations of my own ego-based assumptions: that *I* prefer to be The Most Successful One; that I'm susceptible to equating my worth with my productivity; that a hungry part of me habitually, ineffectively pursues, through ability-based achievements, the unconditional regard I didn't get in my early life.

The most abiding truth that has revealed itself to me through my work is this: Rather than being an indication of thriving, **overachievement is a trauma response**. Overachievement is the trauma response our culture most loves to reward. I don't see how we fight our way out of perverse rewards for trauma responses without spending some time unpacking the feelings our culture expects us to sublimate.

Jealousy is feeling overprotective of what you see as yours, and fearful that someone else will take it. *Envy* is wanting what someone else has and resenting them for having it when you don't. Jealousy is possessive; envy is covetous.

We've all felt these feelings. These are human feelings. They can be so useful if we don't demonize them: **Jealousy and envy point to *what we want*.** We can let these feelings guide us toward the hard work of taking responsibility for our own ambition if we can resist the urge to let them guide us toward punching a friend in the nuts: literally, digitally, or passive-aggressively.

If any of this is resonating, I earnestly recommend you repeat this mantra to yourself daily: **Success is not a zero-sum game.** My dear friend getting a wonderful opportunity from Netflix or Broadway does not diminish a single one of my past accomplishments and does not take a single future accolade away from me.

In fact, best friends Ann Friedman and Aminatou Sow coined the concept of "shine theory" to argue that my friend's success actually *enhances* my own: *I don't shine if you don't shine.* And shine theory works: You were a little impressed to learn that I *know* people affiliated with Netflix and Broadway, right?

For my money, the cardinal text on literary jealousy and envy is Dear Sugar's column "We Are All Savages Inside." Here the prophet Cheryl Strayed writes:

> When you feel like crap because someone has gotten something you want you force yourself to remember how very much you have been given. You remember that there is plenty for all of us. You remember that someone else's success has absolutely no bearing on your own. You remember that a wonderful thing has happened to one of

your literary peers and maybe, if you keep working and if you get lucky, something wonderful may also someday happen to you.

Then, as if the above weren't enough to send me to bed for a week, Strayed personally assassinates me with an even more piercing observation: Jealousy is almost always connected to privilege and entitlement. To be jealous of someone who, say, published an award-winning book by age thirty is to admit that you're someone who imagines yourself capable of that kind of feat. If you're someone who feels a lot of envy, it's probably because you've been given "a tremendous amount of things that you did not earn or deserve."

In short: If news of your friend's success fills your throat with bile, then you have some emotional work to do that isn't directly about writing but will still directly benefit your writing.

I have found over and over again that the way out of the rabbit hole of my own bitterness is relocating childlike joy in creating, making sure I'm taking all possible action that my dreams demand, caring for my nutrition, sleep, and exercise, checking in with my favorite collaborators, having fun with my friends, and reminding myself how gobsmacked my twelve-year-old self would be by my adult life. That list, in a sense, is the recovery program for my addiction to overachievement.

Do you remember your twelve-year-old self? Gangly or pudgy, too tall or too short, stinky and pimpled, totally uncertain about everything, a hapless but enthusiastic blob of potential? Do you remember how wholeheartedly they *loved* getting lost in a book, or a video game, or a TV show? Do you remember how *real* their favorite characters felt to them, how intimately they knew them? Do you remember how they dreamed of going to college, or living in a big city, or having interesting, maybe even *gay*, artist friends? When you work on your dreams, work on behalf of the twelve-year-old you, even if she was, just to choose a random example, a closeted spelling bee nerd sweating through her dress shields. On a regular basis, say to yourself: Dang, just *look* what you pulled off.

The above is hard and rewarding work, and I invite you to engage it in your own ongoing way. But let me also offer one tiny shortcut to enlightenment: When all else fails, remind yourself that every moment in the sun is ultimately nothing more than a moment. No matter how big and buzzy your friend's project is, and I don't care if it rides all the way from the *New York Times* bestseller list to the Academy Awards red carpet, its duration in the public conversation will be *limited*. We simply live in too distracted and overcrowded a multimedia era for any buzz to last very long. Fortunately or not, this will be just as true for your projects as theirs.

So do the hard work of being happy for other people—I can promise you that genuinely enjoying a friend's success makes life better. And on the hard days, close the social media tabs and remember that tomorrow will bring new headlines.

Impostor Syndrome

I told you in the opening chapter of this book how *loud* my impostor syndrome has been since I got a job at Stanford. My impostor syndrome sneers at me: Poser, you got this job because someone wants to blow sunshine up your ass, or because you got dumb-lucky, and surely, imminently, someone more qualified will come along to claim it. (For the record, the feeling I just described also trucks with jealousy.)

Somewhere around my second year in the job, it occurred to

me: If one of my students earned this position, how would I want her to behave in it? Would I want her to act, for years, as if the lottery made a terrible mistake in selecting her? Would I want her to act daffy, stunned, overwhelmed? Would I want her to be so consumed with wondering how she got the job, and when someone would take it away from her, that this wondering diminished her joy in work she loved? Would I wish for her brain to work constantly on the least impressive way to state all her accomplishments, thus seeming to prove how undeserving she is of the position? Would I hope she assumes that every one of her colleagues regards her as an expendable idiot?

You will probably not be too shocked to learn that no, I do not hope that a single one of my students *ever* self-talks that way.

It's too easy to forget that scarcity environments are specifically engineered to make their constituents wonder if they deserve to be there. And every university that brags about its low admissions rate, including my alma mater and my employer, is a scarcity environment.

An especially brilliant graduate student I taught once posed this incisive question: Who wins Stanford? The presence of this question is like a metal detector for a scarcity environment. It's revealing because I have never witnessed a human being take up any version of this question and declare confidently: Me, I am the winner, I bathe in the serenity of my conviction that I deserve to be here, I *know* I am the best one. I was positive I'd get in, and I know innately that I belong here: These are words I have never heard a single student, faculty, or staff member speak about Stanford University.

The unanswerability of this question of "Who wins?" reveals how it keeps us endlessly pedaling: Winning is both impossible and a zero-sum game that necessitates making enemies of every would-be ally. In other words, an unyielding drive to win is one of the most spiritually deadening and socially isolating forces that can exist in a person. And our culture is especially adept at coaching it into people before their frontal lobes have fully developed. I've learned that there are two weeks on campus every year that consistently produce a social crisis: recruiting week for management consultants and the release of the *Forbes* 30 Under 30 list.

I'm reminded of a fact that often wows my students: The Academy Awards were originally devised as a labor-control mechanism. From Sophie Hayssen's 2023 retrospective in *Teen Vogue:* "The desire for industry control also inspired the creation of the Academy Awards in 1929. After a number of scandals, the awards offered an opportunity to generate positive publicity. [Louis B.] Mayer is even quoted in one of his biographies specifically identifying the awards as a means for creative control. He said if he gave filmmakers 'cups and awards, they'd kill themselves to produce what I wanted.'"

Note Mayer's framing here: To a group of people who create images professionally, an award could be perceived as so valuable as to be worth sacrificing one's life.

An addiction to overachievement, powered by impostor syndrome, is the ideal helpmate to this accolade-chasing, zero-sum scarcity model of success: **There's nothing more useful to keeping us desperately striving than the core belief that nothing we'll ever do will be enough.** Awards and hard-won admissions are strategies to keep us striving—and when we're striving for our next gold star, we're usually not advocating for better working conditions for *everybody.*

Also, let's not overlook how much working conditions can affect professional trajectories. In the most-read article in the history of *Harvard Business Review,* "Stop Telling Women They Have Impostor Syndrome," coauthors Ruchika Tulshyan and Jodi-Ann Burey put forth the ground-shifting argument that the crisis of confidence we've named "impostor syndrome" in fact points to the cultural and organizational failure of workplaces to include white women and women of color, rather than pointing to individual failures that must be addressed by the women themselves. They write:

> Even as we know it today, impostor syndrome puts the blame on individuals, without accounting for the historical and cultural contexts that are foundational to how it manifests in both women of color and white women. Impostor syndrome directs our view toward fixing women at work instead of fixing the places where women work.
>
> Even if women demonstrate strength, ambition, and resilience, our daily battles with microaggressions, especially expectations and assumptions formed by stereotypes and racism, often push us down. Impostor syndrome as a concept fails to capture this dynamic and puts the onus on women to deal with the effects. Workplaces remain misdirected toward seeking individual solutions for issues disproportionately caused by systems of discrimination and abuses of power.

So is my impostor syndrome loud inside my head at this university, or is this university loud about its legacy of exclusion? Is the insecurity I've felt the incidental byproduct of my personal impostor syndrome, or is it exactly the intended effect of this university's legacy of exclusion? Am I not prestigious enough, or is the entire concept of prestige racist, sexist, and corrupt? Have I failed to project appropriate confidence, or has my confidence been systematically diminished and punished?

You decide.

Unhealthy Competition

Once upon a time in my bartending era of the early aughts, a boy I used to see decided to bring his new girlfriend into my place of employment. I was—not pleased about this decision. The boy and I had not stopped whatever we were doing together so very long before, nor was I particularly content with that severance. And here he was with this new, gorgeous girl, who had the *audacity* to be another blonde poet from the Midwest, standing at my register, asking for two pints of Brooklyn Lager. I believe that was the first time I'd ever charged him for a beer. I charged him for two.

On a cigarette break some beers later, the blonde poet, who like most women was half my size, sized me up and declared: "You'd look hot with a black eye." To date this is still the most confusingly aggressive thing a woman has ever said to me, except for everything my mother has ever said to me. I believe I replied with "Don't tempt me," which is also both aggressive and confusing. Eventually the poet left with her man, and there I was, a jilted bartender with a punch or two still lodged in the chamber of her fist. (Pop quiz: At that moment, was I feeling jealousy, envy, or both?)

So I did what any reasonable, heartbroken twenty-three-year-old poet would do: I went home and googled the bitch. In doing so, I made the most offensive possible discovery: The poet was talented, celebrated, and repeatedly published. She was *good*. This was *bad*.

Then I did the next most reasonable thing: I submitted poems to almost every single journal that had ever published her.

A month or two later, something truly stunning happened: One of the journals accepted one of my poems.

Years later, at the Association of Writers and Writing Programs conference, I ran into the editor who had published me. I thanked him for that early acceptance and told him it had been very meaningful to me.

He said: "You're so welcome. I was actually on the fence about that poem when I first read it because I'd never heard of you. So, I remember I ran it by The Blonde Poet. She said you were good and I should take it."

At this my jaw hit the floor so hard that I probably still have rugburn scars on my chin. I have no idea what inspired this woman to do me this kindness, but if she ever reads this: You magnificent cunt, thank you.

I like to tell my students: Never underestimate how much of the world's creative output was generated in response to spite, pettiness, or jealousy. I also think that competition can be a tremendously healthy and motivating force—*if* we don't let it spin out of control.

While I would hardly classify a frantic, chain-smoking 4 a.m. internet deep dive of my ex's new flame as "healthy competition," I'm happy to report that while my preoccupation with her didn't persist beyond graduation a few months later, publishing that poem did lead me to publish more. I now see that 4 a.m. deep dive as a crucial moment: I could have let my envy drive me to do something deranged like trying to sabotage her, but instead I let it drive me *toward what I actually wanted,* which was putting my poems out into the world and seeing them appreciated.

I share this embarrassing story because I learned valuable strategy from it. Mainly this: **A talented person who's two to five**

years ahead of you in achieving professional goals can be a far more useful reference point for your career than the luminary who's fifteen to twenty years ahead.

I sometimes call these people "career comps." They can be people you're terribly envious of, and they can also be people you admire. It's possible to read their author websites as repositories of opportunities: Where have they published, what fellowships and residencies have they held, who represents them?

My stormy bout of envy could have led me into tearing another blonde poet down. But for whatever reason, probably nothing more than my ego's desperate hunger for bylines, my ambition led me to emulate her instead. I haven't googled her for years, but I'm certain she's still wildly talented and even more published now. Let your rivalries motivate you without letting them consume you.

Treating Your Body as a Plant Stand for Your Mind*

For too many years, I treated my writing routine as a daily sprint toward the burial plot of a midcentury misogynist. I would sit up in bed, open my computer, hammer out as many pages as possible, cram a quick sandwich in my face only once I was too hungry to function, then hammer out some more pages, crush a Diet Dr. Pepper when my energy flagged, pop some Advil when my head throbbed, and basically never give up until I could not see words anymore. Did I take breaks? Of course! That pack a day of Camel Lights wasn't gonna smoke itself.

---

*   The poet and memoirist Maggie Smith's podcast interview with Prof. Kate Bowler on Bowler's podcast *Everything Happens* is the source of this incredible line and concept.

In this phase of my checkered creative life, exercise, nutrition, sleep hygiene, pacing, or basic regard for the advice of the U.S. Surgeon General just didn't feel as important to me as finishing my next draft by yesterday, if not sooner. Reading this description now, I'm just like: Laura, what fresh Aaron Sorkin hell is this?

The truth is I wasn't thinking. I was *acting*. I was living my entire life in a blind sprint toward a kind of fame and wealth that doesn't exist, or maybe existed for writers only until the late nineties, or almost killed Britney Spears, or did kill Whitney Houston, Marilyn Monroe, and Anthony Bourdain.

Please internalize this before I did: The world is not dying for your draft, and neither should you be.

In my work at the pressure-cooker university, I'd estimate that a student appears in my office hours about once a month in inconsolable tears. My first inquiry is always: Tell me about your eating and sleeping in the last twenty-four to forty-eight hours. And the answer is always something like: I will deserve to eat lunch once I've written twenty more pages, published them as a *New Yorker* cover story, and made the *Forbes* 30 Under 30 list, because I am worthless unless I win this year's social crisis. While silently cursing American capitalism for putting our young people through this kind of psychological wringer, I guide my cherished student toward a sandwich, a nap, and a walk, and then they treat me like some kind of oracle when this helps them feel better.

I am not an oracle. I'm just a girl from Minnesota who learned the hard way that **skipped meals don't earn interest in the creative bank, stagnant bodies can't create moving stories, and real stamina means saving some energy for tomorrow.** You are not God, Wonder Woman, or a machine, and neither am I. If you wish to outlive your sources, rivals, and enemies, then treat your body as you would a beloved friend.

Unrealistic Expectations

Some years ago, I was trying to slip out of a dinner party in a tony suburb about forty-five minutes away from my house in San Francisco. During this attempt, the hostess cornered me and asked, in a loud and irrefutable tone, if I wouldn't mind giving her pregnant friend a ride back to the city. I had only just met this friend; let's call her Dara. I was sleepy and tired of small talk and did not at all want to share the ride home, but the hostess put me in a position where saying no would have entailed being terribly rude to one person who had just fed me dinner and another who was hosting life. And I am from Minnesota. So Dara and I climbed into my Subaru.

Within minutes, Dara's conversation revealed that this ride was a setup. My expectant highway companion, proud to inform me of her elite education and sprawling income, also shared that she was a corporate lawyer who dreamed of transitioning into full-time writing.

A key detail: *I had consented to the ride, but I had not consented to this advisory conversation.* And this has happened to me more times than I can count; someone's granddaughter or niece-in-law or friend is interested in writing, so without even asking my permission, my mother or cousin or friend volunteers me for the free labor of educating a stranger in one of the world's most competitive and badly paid professions. (Friends and relatives of writers: Please stop doing this. A double-opt-in is a blessed thing.) And listen: Obviously I understand how impenetrable the writing world can seem, and clearly I have some interest in offering strangers insights on one of the world's most competitive and badly paid professions! That's why offering these insights is literally my job, *for which I am paid and control my own schedule.*

So it wasn't entirely Dara's fault that I arrived at her conversation so weary; she couldn't know that I'd already been volunteered, much to my resentment, for this kind of conversation five hundred times.

All the same, this iteration of the conversation was not destined for success. Dara spoke in salary lines, asking datemarked questions. And none of my answers pleased her at all. The conversation went something like this:

DARA: What can I expect to make in the first year of writing professionally?

LAURA: Zero dollars. If you get one byline in the first year, you're killing it.

DARA (dismayed): Oh. Okay. What about at five years?

Laura pauses to reflect on the time she was too broke to get on the city bus during the same week her film got into the Tribeca Film Festival. That was, what, about eight years into professional writing? Ten years?

LAURA: Maybe something like five to ten thousand, if you pitch really hard. I recommend maintaining multiple income sources. Writing doesn't operate on the same kind of salary structure as law, medicine, education, sales, tech, or governance.

DARA (mounting rage): I make two hundred and fifty thousand a year now before bonuses. At what point should I expect to make that much money as a writer?

LAURA (stifling uncomfortable laughter): Is that a deer????

This scene continues for forty more minutes.

The mindset I'm trying to highlight is that of **unrealistic expectations**. And let me *not* throw Dara under the Subaru without calling myself out too: As an inexperienced writer, I fully expected that if I worked hard enough, I would publish a book before finishing college, become a bestselling author immediately, defy all the odds, and earn a comfortable living doing only the writing I most wanted to do. I am writing this book explicitly because this kind of mythical thinking is so painfully common.

In my effort to foster realistic expectations, here are some hard financial truths of writing as a career that I have derived from long evidence and experience.

EVEN THE MOST FINANCIALLY SUCCESSFUL WRITERS RARELY EARN ENOUGH TO CHANGE CLASS OUTCOMES FOR OTHER PEOPLE IN THEIR FAMILY. I have two dependents in one of the most expensive metro areas in the country, so I teach at a wealthy university for steady income and health insurance. I would not be able to support anybody else, such as aging parents, on my current salary, which includes income from teaching, publishing, and speaking. I categorically do not recommend that anyone with dependents rely on freelance writing income alone, and I want everyone to know that writing is not the kind of career that is likely to allow you to pay off your mom's mortgage or your siblings' student loans. For more reading on this, Nicole Chung's excellent memoir *A Living Remedy* provides a candid and sobering account of literary class realities for working-class families.

WRITERS ALMOST NEVER EARN A CONSISTENT INCOME YEAR-OVER-YEAR FROM WRITING. Dara's expectation of making $250,000 a year might be possible if you sold a book *and* its TV rights in a single year. But this would be one extraordinary year, not *every* year. Also, most book advances are paid out in thirds or quarters throughout a book's publication pipeline, so even if you shoot the moon and sell for $250,000, that probably means you'll get $62,500 on signing, $62,500 on delivery of the manuscript, $62,500 at the time of publication, and $62,500 a year *after* publication. But don't forget your agent's 15 percent cut! You're actually getting four installments of $53,125, totaling $212,500. But the IRS wants their cut too! At the current freelancer tax rate of about 30 percent, that means that your take-home income from a shoot-the-moon $250K book deal is $148,750, paid in installments distributed across one or several years. And that deal may keep you so busy it takes you five years to generate your next project. And you probably want to do your best to put that shoot-the-moon advance toward a down payment on a house, because that lump sum likely won't come again. Sorry, Dara.

WRITERS RARELY HIT MAJOR FINANCIAL SUCCESS EARLY, IF AT ALL. Most of us need years to find and grow into our voices, to gain life experience worth writing about, and to make income-generating connections. This reality does not position us well to pay off student loans, buy homes, or hit other milestones of financial stability until later into adulthood, if at all. (A large cadre of poets is laughing in my face at the prospect that they will *ever* be able to own a home purchased with writing income.) This is different from other high-risk, high-reward careers: Because their employability depends on the agility of youth, a gifted actor or athlete might earn change-your-life money right out of the gate. A writer's employability relies on discernment, diplomacy, wisdom, and eloquence, and these are the gifts of age. This is yet another good argument for taking care of your health: So you can live long enough to enjoy these gifts, and outlive the sources of your stories (more on page 201).

NO MATTER HOW TALENTED YOU ARE, SOME GENRES ARE EASIER TO MONETIZE THAN OTHERS. I mentioned in chapter 4 that my personal experience has revealed nonfiction to be much easier to monetize than fiction or poetry. I also wish someone had told me candidly that within the big tent of fiction, "genre" fiction, specifically, romance, fantasy, sci-fi, mystery, and young-adult generate distinctly more money than "literary" fiction. While considering all that, I think it's valuable to know that self-published authors take home a much larger royalty share of their sales than traditionally published authors do, even if that also means they bear the publicity, marketing, and distribution load without support. And, of course, screenwriters can earn as much in a week on a union TV writing job, or in a few months on a development deal, as poets, fiction writers, playwrights, or journalists take home in a year. These are all financial realities that have nothing to do with talent and everything to do with distribution, audience, and scale, and they're worth understanding as you chart your path.

EVEN THE MOST SUCCESSFUL WRITERS DO NOT EARN A LIVING FROM A SINGLE SOURCE. John Grisham? Was an attorney for years. Michael Crichton? A full-ass medical doctor, like William Carlos Williams. T. S. Eliot worked as a bank teller. Toni Morrison's days in the early 1970s consisted of rising before dawn to write her first book, *The Bluest Eye,* getting her two sons to school, then working full-time as an editor at Random House, where she published Angela Davis and Toni Cade Bambara. (Morrison published her debut at age thirty-nine, and these facts are better than espresso to me.) Maya Angelou was a dancer, actress, producer, director, activist, sex worker, professor, teen mother, and the first Black woman streetcar operator in San Francisco. Even Stephen King, who has published sixty-five novels and sold more than four hundred million copies of them, owns a radio station— and has also expressed a lot of candid regret about how much cocaine he consumed in the early chapters of his career. Writers have to be multitalented, versatile, curious, resilient, and nimble just to survive. There is no shame or failure in day jobs, side hustles, or commercial work. Broad, eclectic knowledge bases make great storytellers.

Calluses, Not Shortcuts

Both Dara's story and my own demonstrate a strong desire for a shortcut. If I'm prodigious and prolific enough, the naivete of ego asks, don't I get to skip the line?

During one particular discussion in my undergraduate section of Pitching and Publishing, the class and I got to talking about BookTok. These young, hungry digital natives could chart how books were selling or bestselling after going viral on TikTok, and they wanted my tips for doing the same.

"Okay," I said. "Who's ever had an experience of going viral before?"

None of the students had had a published story go viral, but a few of them had seen tweets or posts take off.

"How did that feel?" I asked.

Weird. Unsettling. Exposed. Time-sucking. Judgy. The sensation of being watched, like eyes on the back. Not actually that fun.

I love these students and ribbing them is always tantamount to ribbing myself: They can hardly name an unreasonable aspiration that has never kept me up at night. And as previously discussed, a calculated social media strategy that results in going viral on BookTok can be a phenomenal marketing asset.

But what these relatively inexperienced writers couldn't see is that **watching something you made unexpectedly meet a *very* large quantity of eyeballs is both desirable and *stressful*.** People will make a lot of comments on your creation, and some of those comments will be ungenerous or unkind. The ten thousand sincere compliments will roll off your back and the five searing critiques will live rent-free in your head. Dumbasses will snitch-tag you in the critiques. Someone might spot an opportunity in publishing a counterpoint to your story, or a digest of the backlash against it, and then you might have to watch that go viral too. Going viral can be lucrative in certain ways, yes, but it can also be surprisingly painful.

None of this is to say that we shouldn't strive to write universal stories that make a lot of people think and feel or that we shouldn't develop creative social media marketing strategies. But I *am* arguing that **you will be best prepared to meet this maelstrom of internet-scale thoughts on your four-hundred-page book once you've collected plenty of experience processing that public feedback on four-hundred-word and four-thousand-word stories.** Editors give book deals to writers with large piles of clips because those writers have demonstrated that they can connect with an audience, and also because those writers have demonstrated they can *survive* having an audience. The single most maddening aspect of writing as a career, which has wrestled me to the ground basically every day of my life in it, is that **there are no shortcuts.**

Once you collect that experience, you'll learn how to treat yourself in these exposed moments. I know not to plan for a whole lot of productivity on a day a story goes online. I know when to close social media and go touch grass. I know not to snitch-tag. These are calluses I've built from zapping my hand on the third rail of the internet many times, over many years. Before you launch your big book into the world, build some of your own.

Learn When to Walk Away

Part of the way I learned negotiation was by fighting my parents on curfews. The other way was by producing an independent film.

I negotiated around one hundred contracts for *Farah Goes Bang*'s cast, crew, locations, releases, licensing, distribution, and much more. The highest-stakes contract showdown happened just one week out from production.

Picture it: It's May 2012. My friends Meera (director/co-writer) and Paul (cinematographer) are graduating from film school at the University of Southern California. Meera and I have spent the last two years writing more than twenty drafts of the script and have just survived the crowdfunding campaign to fund it. Meera has savvily recruited an entire crew of film students and recent grads to help us shoot. We have just finished casting our three starring roles, thank God, because we're slated to start principal photography next week. My lifetime total experience as a film producer consists of little more than Meera squinting at me over a beer and saying, "You're organized and good with money, you could be a film producer." Blood pressure is running high. I am working *hard* to conceal the fact that I have no idea what I'm doing.

We are walking into a celebratory graduation brunch with Meera and Paul's families when I get a call from someone claiming to be a lawyer newly representing one of the actresses we've just cast. Allow me to paraphrase our conversation.

That's strange that you represent this actress, I say, because two weeks ago I negotiated a whole signed contract for her with a representative who was—not you.

She fired that guy, the lawyer says, and I'm the new gun in this saloon. Also, she won't be getting out of bed for a penny less than three times the figure you negotiated two weeks ago.

My heart plummets into my stomach and out of my butt. The figure this lawyer has just named is half of our total production budget; there is no way we can meet it. We'd been excited about this actress. And we're shooting next week.

I hang up, numb and buzzing. I go back into the restaurant, tell Meera what's going on, apologize to the families, shove three bites of eggs Benedict into my mouth, and go back out to the sidewalk to make more panicky calls. One of those calls goes to my then-husband Patrick, to whom I have been married for less than a year. I explain the situation.

Laura, he says, you're in Los Angeles. From where you're standing right now, you could spit and hit one hundred other qualified actresses. Why are you panicking? Just find someone else.

But I liked *this* actress, I explain, because she's internet-famous in this one specific way, and she was funny when we met her, and we're a week out from production.

But you have to remember the bedrock rule of negotiation, Patrick says. The person who is willing to walk away holds all the power.

It dawns on me that I *am* standing within one hundred feet of one hundred other qualified actresses, and I *can* find another one in less than a week. People do that all the time. It dawns on me that if I give in to this new gun in the saloon once, I'll only have shown him that he can push me around, and then what's to stop him from tripling the rate again? It dawns on me that one of our leads getting paid three times more than her coequals could lead to tension on set. All of a sudden, I can clearly see the path that proceeds by walking away from this petty little shitbird of a lawyer.

Oh my god, I say to Pat, you're right.

I know, Pat says. So call that dickhead back and tell him he just lost his client her first starring role in a feature.

I return to brunch again. I update the whole table; everyone is invested by now. Meera and the table cosign the strategy of telling the bad lawyer to go kick rocks and finding a new lead within a week.

I return to my new office, a South Central sidewalk, once again. This emotional roller coaster is traveling fast, and shortly after receiving one of the worst phone calls of my life, now I get to make one of the greatest phone calls of my life.

Hello, lawyer, I say. We will not be signing your new contract. You can go ahead and inform your new client that you just torpedoed her first starring role in a feature film.

This mofo hits the *ceiling*. First he tries condescension: Listen, I know you want to be a film producer, I'm trying to help you out when I tell you that this isn't how it works.

I *am* a film producer, I say with all the unearned confidence of youthful hubris challenged. And right now *you're* the one sucking at your job.

Next he tries aggression: We had these dates blocked out, so you're liable for lost wages. We'll sue.

Marvelous, I say. Talk to my lawyer. Bye.

No orgasm has ever blasted me higher than hanging up on that guy. He did threaten to sue our production lawyer, who laughed in his face: Clearly *we* were not the ones in breach of contract. I never returned a single one of his calls ever again. We did not work with his client. We absolutely found a brilliant actress to fill the role in time, and she remains one of my favorite people. That lawyer may have ruined brunch, but because we were more willing to handle a few days of casting uncertainty than months to years of working with a dickhead, he couldn't ruin our movie.

It will be your job, as an artist, to hold on tight to many things: your sanity, stamina, self-confidence, and savviest collaborators. It will also be your job to know when to walk away. Never forget that real power is built on both.

Here are some other common instances where a savvy writer will likely be best served by walking away:

- A collaboration isn't working. I just feel like this coauthor, editor, or agent doesn't get it, in a nagging way that won't leave me alone. Or: This collaborator and I are fundamentally working toward divergent, irreconcilable goals. Or: This collaborator is not doing what they said they'd do, so I can't trust them.
- The rate doesn't fit the task. No, I cannot reasonably read and evaluate fifty different twenty-page submissions for a nonnegotiable stipend of $100. No, I can't turn around one thousand researched words in twenty-four hours for $50.
- The project was misrepresented. You told me (or, better yet, my signed contract told me) this would be four days of work for $1,000, but it's been three months and no light has appeared at the end of this tunnel.
- I got an offer I cannot refuse. This freelance $1,000 project has been fun, but I just received an unexpected offer for a desirable full-time job, and I can't do both, so I have to go with the more lucrative opportunity.

Other People's Stories

The most tantalizing baubles in a writer's life can be the stories that don't belong to us. They glitter. They gleam. They arouse our envy *and* our jealousy. They make our fingers itch. Couldn't we just?

Let me give you some handy examples. Some people I may or may not have known in high school may or may not have put a FIRE SALE, EVERYTHING MUST GO sign on the lawn of a local crematorium. I might know some people who might have made some money, hypothetically, in the sex and drug trades. I might have two different friends who each had a parent who was a clergy member vowed to celibacy . . . until meeting their other parent. This sort of story is catnip to me: This person was so smoking hot you were literally willing to risk *eternal damnation*? I would bug a therapist's office just to learn the details of that relationship's first act, but even if I managed that, the story would never belong to me.

I won't pretend I haven't been tempted. All these good people have been taunting me for years with scenes that include character, conflict, plot, setting, *and* soundtrack. And during those years, they've also loved me, fed me, housed me, and demonstrated their deep preference for privacy. So I respect this borderline. I encourage you to cultivate people in your life to whom your loyalty is greater than your ambition.

It is pure inevitability that your writing ambitions will eventually collide with a story that is not yours to tell, or a story that is very much yours to tell but will upset someone if you tell it. It is extremely likely that you will learn the locations of some of these borderlines by crossing them. Entire books have been written on literary ethics, particularly the ethics of nonfiction, and Melissa Febos's *Body Work* is one of my favorites. But for the purposes of this emergency chapter, I will break down the most common advice I give to my students.

CHANGE THE NAMES. In any kind of creative writing—personal nonfiction, fiction, scripting—change them all. Change them even if you're writing something you think is flattering. Change as many identifying details as you can. If you are reporting a strictly journalistic piece, you may need to attribute all quotes, so speak to people who are willing to speak on the record, use initials and middle names where necessary, and in the case of that necessity, make sure you have editorial support for your sources' privacy. Ethics are a matter of choosing battles, and in personal essays, names are usually an easy one to concede; they are harder in reporting.

OUTLIVE THE BASTARDS. Except in cases where a large estate protected by named executors succeeds them, dead people cannot sue. Remember my previous point about taking care of your health?

FACT-CHECK WITHIN AN INCH OF YOUR LIFE. Preferably this is done through your publisher. You may have to pay for it yourself. Fact-checking is to litigation what birth control is to unplanned pregnancy or prenuptial agreement to divorce: not free, but dramatically cheaper than the outcome it prevents. Libel and slander suits both address *false* statements committed to the public record. You guard against them by proving, to the greatest extent possible, that what you say is provable and true.

MAKE YOUR FIRST DRAFT RUTHLESS, AND YOUR FINAL DRAFT PUBLISHABLE. Writing an early draft is hard enough without worrying about other people, so I advise my students to get the first draft down on paper without considering anybody else's feelings. Omit nothing as you generate and form the story. Then, as you move into the editing stage, isolate the material that you think might upset someone, and make decisions about what to do with this material on a case-by-case basis.

I run anxious as a person, and my educated guess is that this is also probably true about a person who would be inclined to buy this book and read through its final chapter. Anxiety's impact on the process I just described usually goes like this: I imagine a story and immediately assume everyone will hate me for it. Then I work up enough courage to write two drafts of the story and see that, actually, one stolen quote on page 2 and one snarky aside on page 6 are likely to offend someone I know. I realize that cutting the snarky aside and anonymizing the quote don't diminish the storytelling at all. Or I run the quote by its speaker via email, provide some context for why I've used it, and ask their permission to use it while also sincerely remaining open to cutting it.

There will be drafts you scrap because the personal cost simply isn't worth it, and there will be drafts you decide are worth the trouble. A professional's work is learning to tell the difference.

Feuds, Apologies, and Reconciliations

By now you know me as a person with loud opinions, demented ambition, and at least one divorce under my belt. My garishly strange résumé includes experience working as a New York City bartender, being a classroom teacher in a maximum-security prison, and delivering a nearly nine-pound baby without an epidural. I've had many tussles with jealousy, competition, and ego. Playgrounds taunted me with the moniker "Human Dictionary." Manhattan drinkers taunted me with "Fuck you, bitch." I've spent decades in a career that requires a certain level of, well, delusion.

My point is that writers, writ large, are socially disastrous. We prefer the company of the imaginary to the real. We disappear for long, unannounced stretches. We steal everything from snippets of conversation to childhood wounds. We exhume pain you thought was buried generations ago. We live with egos that vacillate between telling us we're a genius and telling us we're dog poop. We always have homework. Serially we commit the profoundly unfair act of committing our version of the story to paper, thus privileging our perspective over everyone else's.

What all this adds up to is that I have had to do some hard work on **reconciliation and apology**. Briefly, I considered including here a list of all the literary sins I have ever had to apologize for committing, but that list would transform this book into a legally dicey, multivolume compendium with at least one fatality (me).

I have a big mouth, but to the best of my knowledge I don't have scores of enemies, largely because I have learned that **most of the time, an apology costs nothing and can bloom into a surprising gift.** This principle has produced one especially beautiful result in my life.

I have an old friend from grad school to whom I refer affectionately as a "poetry bruiser." He once threatened to fight a visiting writer for using the term *crack house* in a poem. He was fond of and well acquainted with my salty bartender persona. He's brilliant, sharp-tongued, and loves poetry more than almost anyone I've ever met. It's a sacred matter to him, a calling. I have so much respect for this stance: for its total lack of pragmatism, for its fervor, for its tenderness.

I was about a week away from moving from New York to San Francisco when I attended a party at the Bowery Poetry Club and ran into Poetry Bruiser. I had just signed with the agent who would sell my young adult novel. I guess word had gotten out about that, because the first words Poetry Bruiser greeted me with were "What's all this I hear about this Judy Blume bullshit?"

Here's the thing. I can take a ribbing. I love to shit-talk in good fun. But in my personal code of conduct, you cannot be a man, *and* take a shit on my first book deal, *and also* take a shit on her royal highness Judy Blume. That is just not a combination I can abide.

I don't think I even summoned a retort. I just glared hard, turned heel, and walked out. I was furious, and my feelings were so hurt. Have you ever heard that writers are socially disastrous?

I moved to California, I wrote the young adult novel, and life mostly moved on. It occurred to me now and then, though I hardly allowed myself to acknowledge the thought, that I missed my old friend Poetry Bruiser. It occurred to me that if I hadn't happened to move across the country a week after our Bowery dust-up, we probably would have run into each other at another party a month later and laughed about it. But, instead, we didn't speak for five years.

The spring I was finishing *Farah Goes Bang*, I happened to confide to a mutual poet friend some grief that Poetry Bruiser had never apologized for his unkind comment. And the poet friend said something that surprised me: "I think his fear was that you would abandon your poetry."

This comment completely recolored the interaction to me. I had thought that Poetry Bruiser had taken offense to my publishing a YA novel because he felt egotistically defensive of *his* allegiance to poetry. But what I failed to realize was that his comment was meant to be protective of *my* allegiance to poetry. And in this new light, there was something in that impulse that I found very, very sweet.

I decided to write to Poetry Bruiser. I wrote that I'd regretted the end of our friendship, that our mutual friend had helped shed some new light on the conflict, and that I was truly sorry for my part in the long silence.

He responded almost immediately, warmly confirming his support of my work, and we have been friends again ever since.

This would be a nice reconciliation story on its own, and I offered my apology with no expectations. I couldn't know that Poetry Bruiser, in his abiding passion, would found, fund, and launch his own poetry press. I couldn't know that he would publish my first book of poems, *Become a Name*.

But he did.

So take it from me: If you ever feel an unissued apology disturbing your rest, if an unresolved conflict still tugs at you years later, even if you are *positive* the other person was the bigger asshole, if there is any *shadow* of a chance that you were a little bit of a storming-out asshole too, just apologize.

An apology costs nothing and can bloom into a surprising gift.

Fortune Favors the Bold

Have I told you the story of how that young adult novel came to be? It's one of my favorites.

The year, as in the previous story, is 2008. I am finishing grad school and living in the former Jewish Hospital of Brooklyn, now gentrification-in-progress apartments in Prospect Heights, Brooklyn. It is important to note this as the pre–economic crash *Twilight* era, when young adult fiction was a hugely growing sector of publishing, and the undead were basically tentpoling the entire industry. I'd heard water cooler chatter that a dear and brilliant friend of mine from both college and grad school, Yvonne Woon, had just signed with a literary agent and sold a six-figure, multi-book YA deal. (Shout-out to the fantastic books Yvonne and this deal produced, *Dead Beautiful, Life Eternal,* and *Love Reborn,* and to her most recent page-turner, Edgar Award finalist *My Flawless Life.*)

The agent's name was Ted Malawer, and he was another college classmate of Yvonne's and mine. This worked out really well when Ted happened to come to a party I was hosting with my roommates at the Jewish Hospital.

Against the din of the party, Ted and I shop-talked about how great Yvonne was and how exciting her deal was. He asked me if I had ever thought about writing young adult fiction.

Some other important notes: While I had been an avid consumer of YA fiction since I'd figured out how to sneak into that library section around age six, I had never, up to this moment, spent a single moment of my life considering writing a young adult novel. I was getting an MFA in poetry, I had written and produced two stage plays, and I had written *maybe* one short story for an intro-level undergrad writing workshop. I had literally zero experience writing fiction.

So, what did I say?

I said, my god, I think about writing YA fiction all the time. I can't *stop* thinking about it. I lie awake at night consumed by it. I am convinced that my destiny lies ahead, in a young adult novel.

Ted, surprised but pleased, asked me what kind of YA fiction concepts, exactly, had me up all night.

Well, I said, stalling for time as I rifled through my repository of ideas, I think it would be cool to write a book about four high school girls who start a hip-hop crew, and the two co-MCs fall in love.

Let's have lunch, Ted said.

Luckily, I had enough good sense to flesh out my idea more between the party and the lunch. Ted and I met up just before my MFA graduation, he signed me as a client, and he instructed me to write something like the first three to five chapters of the book. I wrote the chapters over the summer, and we sold them as a partial manuscript in fall 2008.

The moral of the story: **When an interesting person offers an opportunity you don't fully understand, but your intuition still senses a door cracking open, then I don't care how underqualified, terrified, or desperate you might feel, just *kick*.** Kick as hard as you can. You can figure out where to put your foot down later. Kick.

That book didn't make me a bestselling author, a celebrity, or a millionaire. It didn't land me an interview with Oprah, although my mother did personally write Ellen DeGeneres a strongly worded letter about how much she would love it. But it sure did make me a published novelist. It sure did get me my first literary agent—who was such a mensch that I'm proud to mention his name here, even though we eventually, amicably parted ways. And it led to many other intangible gains that I will treasure forever. Here are some of my favorites:

I got to cohost a *Sister Mischief* event at my hometown library—in the very building where my child self snuck into the YA section!—with my high school AP English teacher, the most honorable Betsy Cussler. This was attended by an entire ensemble cast of *This Is Your Life*. One of my mom's bridge friends wondered aloud why the book had to have so many curse words. The smartest question in the Q&A came from an old spelling bee rival. Just picturing Ms. Cussler's copy of my gay little book, all dog-eared and margin-noted, still chokes me up.

At one of our Tribeca screenings of *Farah Goes Bang*, a woman stood up, took the Q&A mic, and said "Hi. My name is Farah, and I'm Iranian American, and I graduated from college in 2004. And no one *ever* makes movies about me. So I just wanted to say thank you." That one comment meant more to me than any ticket we sold or award we won.

Remember he who had the balls to bring his new girlfriend into my bar? Some years later, he also spent an entire day personally chauffeuring my ass to three different book events in an area where I didn't know anyone else. He married another poet from the Midwest. We're fond old friends.

One of those events was at a high school gay-straight alliance. As it wrapped up, a young woman who seemed nervous but engaged came up to talk to me. Avoiding eye contact, with rehearsed nonchalance, she said, "Yeah, I made my mom read your book too, and it helped her understand my coming out, or whatever."

I barely made it back to the car before I started full-body sobbing.

What I'm telling you is this: Your versions of these moments are waiting for you on the other side of a lot of work that, if you're doing it right, will bring you to your knees more than once.

The good news is: You are the only person who can get you to those moments.

The bad news is: You are the only person who can get you to those moments.

Eyes on the page. Ass in the chair.

Keep going. Keep going. Keep going.

FURTHER READING

Throughout this book, I've mentioned a handful of other craft books I've found especially helpful to my creative and capitalistic processes. Here is a complete list of my favorite recommendations for additional reading! (Note: Because the craft of writing is so interlinked with the art of living, this list interprets "craft book" quite broadly.)

Attenberg, Jami. *1000 Words: A Writer's Guide to Staying Creative, Productive, and Focused All Year Round*. New York: Simon and Schuster / Simon Element, 2024.

Chee, Alexander. *How to Write an Autobiographical Novel*. New York: Mariner / Houghton Mifflin Harcourt, 2018.

Febos, Melissa. *Body Work: The Radical Power of Personal Narrative*. New York: Catapult Books, 2022.

Heilbrun, Carolyn. *Writing a Woman's Life*. New York: Women's Press, 1989.

Highsmith, Patricia. *Plotting and Writing Suspense Fiction.* New York: St. Martin's Griffin, 2001.

Lamott, Anne. *Bird by Bird: Some Instructions on Writing and Life.* New York: Vintage, 1995.

Martin, Manjula, ed. *Scratch: Writers, Money, and the Art of Making a Living.* New York: Simon and Schuster, 2017.

Maum, Courtney. *Before and After the Book Deal: A Writer's Guide to Finishing, Publishing, Promoting, and Surviving Your First Book.* New York: Catapult Books, 2020.

Salesses, Matthew. *Craft in the Real World: Rethinking Fiction Writing and Workshopping.* New York: Catapult Books, 2021.

Strayed, Cheryl. *Tiny Beautiful Things: Advice on Love and Life from Dear Sugar.* New York: Knopf Doubleday, 2012.

Vachon, Christine. *Shooting to Kill: How an Independent Producer Blasts Through the Barriers to Make Movies That Matter.* New York: William Morrow Paperbacks, 1998.

Warner, John. *The Writer's Practice: Building Confidence in Your Nonfiction Writing.* New York: Penguin Books, 2019.

WORKS CITED

Bowler, Kate, host. "Maggie Smith: This Place Could Be Beautiful, Right?" *Everything Happens with Kate Bowler,* podcast, season 10, episode 9, April 7, 2023. https://kate bowler.com/podcasts/this-place-could-be-beautiful-right/.

Chee, Alexander. *How to Write an Autobiographical Novel: Essays.* New York: Mariner / Houghton Mifflin Harcourt, 2018.

Febos, Melissa. *Body Work: The Radical Power of Personal Narrative.* New York: Catapult Books, 2022.

———. "Do You Want to Be Known for Your Writing, or for Your Swift Email Responses?" *Catapult,* March 23, 2017.

Hayssen, Sophie. "The Oscars in Labor History: Union-Busting Is at the Roots of the Ceremony." *Teen Vogue,* March 10, 2023. https://www.teenvogue.com/story/oscars-union-busting.

Maum, Courtney. *Before and After the Book Deal: A Writer's Guide to Finishing, Publishing, Promoting, and Surviving Your First Book.* New York: Catapult Books, 2022.

Smith, Ben. *Traffic: Genius, Rivalry, and Delusion in the Billion-Dollar Race to Go Viral.* New York: Penguin, 2024.

Strayed, Cheryl. "Dear Sugar, the Rumpus Advice Column #69: We Are All Savages Inside." *The Rumpus,* March 31, 2011. https://therumpus.net/2011/03/31/dear-sugar-the-rumpus-advice-column-69-we-are-all-savages-inside/.

Tulshyan, Ruchika, and Jodi-Ann Burey. "Stop Telling Women They Have Impostor Syndrome." *Harvard Business Review,* February 11, 2021. https://hbr.org/2021/02/stop-telling-women-they-have-impostor-syndrome.

ACKNOWLEDGMENTS

It takes a village to raise a book, and I am notably grateful to the following Village People:

My visionary agents Amanda Orozco and Brenna English-Loeb, who believed in me enough to sign me on sample chapters alone.

My brilliant editor Julie Bennett, HBIC of Ten Speed Press, fellow daughter of the prairies.

My family: my sons, Jed and Luke, who light up my life and offer me every incentive to double the quote. My cousins Stephanie DeCesare Schon, MBA, Dr. Barbara DeCesare May, PhD, and Dr. Karen DeCesare Doll, PsyD, who role-modeled female professional ambition in completely badass forms. My parents, who now have proof curfews taught me something.

Dina Gonzalez, who watched over my babies so I could write this one. Te quiero siempre.

The grand witches: Jess Fisher, Kelsey Oakes, Coreen Kopper, Amy Bell. Erica Fishman, whose conversation has made me richer and wiser for thirty years. Anthony Ocampo: Our economy of favors could have a GDP someday. Adrian Van Young: Professional wellness forever!

The all-you-can-eat brilliance buffet of Catapult in the late 2010s: Julie Buntin, Nicole Chung, Matt Ortile, Colin Drohan. Betsy Cussler, That Teacher, who moved her lunch hour to critique a terrified sixteen-year-old's poems. Timothy Donnelly, That Professor, who admitted a mouthy junior to his Senior Honors poetry workshop, told her to get an MFA, then patiently explained what an MFA was.

Sara Blachman, for squinting at me over a spliff in 2005 and declaring, "You're hot, you could be a bartender." Meera Menon, for squinting at me over a beer in 2009 and declaring, "You're organized and good with money, you could be a film producer." Chloe Caldwell, for squinting at me over a CBD honeystick in 2016 and declaring, "*You* should teach that, I'm gonna give you an email address."

Adrian Daub, for squinting at me across a Catapult chat room in 2017 and declaring, "We really need this class at Stanford, I'm going to bring you in as a guest speaker." R. Lanier Anderson, for inventing my dream job with a phone call, mentoring me into it, and changing my life. My Public Humanities dream team: Natalie Jabbar, Mark Greif, Blakey Vermeule, and Jeff Schwegman.

Every single alum of my class "Pitching and Publishing for Popular Media": I am always rooting for you.

And to everyone who worked on this book: Andrea Lau, Ashley Pierce, Dan Myers, Elisabeth Magnus, Ann Roberts, Miriam Taveras, Joey Lozada, and Lauren Chung.

INDEX

ABOUT THE AUTHOR

LAURA GOODE is the author of a collection of poems, *Become a Name*, and a young adult novel, *Sister Mischief*, which was a Best of the Bay pick by the *San Francisco Bay Guardian* and a selection of two American Library Association honor lists. With director Meera Menon, she wrote and produced the feature film *Farah Goes Bang*, which premiered at the Tribeca Film Festival and won the inaugural Nora Ephron Prize from Tribeca and *Vogue*. Her nonfiction writing has appeared in *BuzzFeed Reader*, *New Republic*, *New York Magazine*, *Longreads*, *ELLE*, *Glamour*, *Catapult*, *Refinery29*, and elsewhere. She received her BA and MFA from Columbia University, teaches at Stanford University, and lives in San Francisco.

TEN SPEED PRESS
An imprint of the Crown Publishing Group
A division of Penguin Random House LLC
1745 Broadway
New York, NY 10019
tenspeed.com
penguinrandomhouse.com

A Ten Speed Press Trade Paperback Original

Portions of the introduction were original published in *Catapult* as the essays "How Publishing My First Novel at 25 Almost Ruined My Life" and "Don't Submit. Pitch."

Typefaces: Adobe's Minion, URW Type Foundrys Nimbus Mono, Mostardesign's Sofia Pro, Font Bureau's Benton Modern

Library of Congress Cataloging-in-Publication Data

Names: Goode, L. (Laura), 1983– author
Title: Pitch craft : the writer's guide to getting agented, published, and paid / Laura Goode.
Description: Emeryville : Ten Speed Press, 2025. | Includes bibliographical references and index.
Identifiers: LCCN 2024044062 (print) | LCCN 2024044063 (ebook) | ISBN 9780593837122 trade paperback | ISBN 9780593837139 ebook
Subjects: LCSH: Authorship—Vocational guidance | Authorship—Marketing
Classification: LCC PN153 .G66 2025 (print) | LCC PN153 (ebook) | DDC 070.5/2—dc23/eng/20250511
LC record available at https://lccn.loc.gov/2024044062
LC ebook record available at https://lccn.loc.gov/2024044063

ISBN 978-0-593-83712-2
eBook ISBN 978-0-593-83713-9

Editor: Julie Bennett | Production editor: Ashley Pierce
Designer: Andrea Lau
Production: Dan Myers
Copyeditor: Elisabeth Magnus | Proofreaders: Ann Roberts and Miriam Taveras
Indexer: Ken DellaPenta
Publicist: Lauren Chung | Marketer: Joey Lozada

Manufactured in the U.S.A.

1st Printing

The authorized representative in the EU for product safety and compliance is Penguin Random House Ireland, Morrison Chambers, 32 Nassau Street, Dublin D02 YH68, Ireland, https://eu-contact.penguin.ie.

Cover and title page art piece by Adobe Stock/t1m0n344